Maximising Sales

Terry Melaugh

Copyright © 2014 Terry Melaugh

All rights reserved. This book, or any portion thereof, may not be reproduced, stored in a retrieval system, copied or transmitted in any form or by any means, electronic or mechanical, including scanning, photocopying, recording or otherwise transmitted without the prior written permission of the author. You must not circulate this book in any format.

Disclaimer

This is an information guide. It is not intended as a substitute for legal or other professional services.

While every effort has been made to make this guide accurate, it may contain typographical or content errors. The information expressed herein is the opinion of the author. No responsibility or liability for loss caused to any individual or organisation acting or refraining from action as a result of the material in this publication can be accepted by the publishers or the author.

Maximising Sales

Contents

Introduction 6

Chapter 1. Qualities of a successful salesperson 8

Chapter 2. The importance of proper communication.............17

Chapter 3. Setting Goals 24

Chapter 4. Time management..37

Chapter 5. Why people buy 40

Chapter 6. The sales cycle 46

Chapter 7. Finding new business..50

Chapter 8. The nature of your customer base 54

Chapter 9. Obtaining referrals 60

Chapter 10. Establishing contact 69

Chapter 11. Qualifying the prospect 79

Chapter 12. Identifying needs and wants 84

Chapter 13. Written proposals..98

Chapter 14. Presenting the product 101

Chapter 15. Dealing with objections 125

Chapter 16. Typical objections 135

Chapter 17. Buying signals 144

Chapter 18. Responding to buying signals 149

Chapter 19. Negotiating 152

Chapter 20. Closing the sale 158

Chapter 21. Closing techniques 165

Chapter 22. When things go wrong 182

Chapter 23. Mistakes to avoid 184

Chapter 24. Overcome setbacks 192

Chapter 25. Staying on course 202

Chapter 26. Dealing with the competition 210

Chapter 27. Looking after existing customers 212

Chapter 28. Customer service 222

Chapter 29. Dealing with customer complaints 230

Chapter 30. Key account management 235

Chapter 31. Sales tools and documentation 237

Chapter 32. Leading a sales team 240

Introduction

This book outlines all the techniques you need to employ to succeed in sales. You will be shown how to increase your sales. You will learn how to become more productive. You will be shown how to focus on the important issue of building relationships with your customers and generating sales. You will discover how to set goals and work towards them. You will learn how to overcome setbacks and stay on track. You will understand how to communicate with and influence customers.

Whether you are new to a sales career or just want to increase your sales this book is for you. All of the common sales techniques are distilled in this guide. This book is full of practical tips on how to develop your interpersonal skills and reach your true potential. All of the advice in this book is specific and targeted towards you maximising your sales.

You will be taken through each stage of the sales cycle. You will learn how to get new leads and referrals. You will be shown the best way to handle cold calls. You will learn how to build rapport with prospective customers. You will learn how to overcome the most common objections. You will be shown how to give a successful presentation. You will be shown all the most common methods of closing the sale. You will learn which closing technique to apply in any given situation. You will learn how to negotiate the best deal for your company.

You will learn how to lead the customer to the sale. You will learn to recognise all of the typical buying signals in terms of customer body language, customer speech pattern, customer behaviour and what the customer actually says.

You will be shown the importance of communicating with and looking after customers.
You will be shown why people buy. You will be shown how to get additional business from various sources. You will be shown how to retain customers and increase your business with them. You will learn how to deal with the competition.

You will be shown how to deal with customer complaints. You will be shown how to provide an excellent level of customer service.

You will be given practical examples of what to do and say as well as how to behave. You will learn what to say, how to say it and when to say it. You will also learn what not to say or do. You will learn how to avoid mistakes and what to do when things go wrong. The common pitfalls are pointed out and advice is given on how to avoid these.

You will learn how to lead a sales team and get the optimum performance from them. You will learn how to delegate your work effectively. Most of all you will learn how to maximise your sales.

Chapter 1. Qualities of a successful salesperson

You can learn, practise and develop every single skill that you need to be a successful salesperson. This book will take you through this process, providing practical tips at each stage. If you put these guidelines into practice, you will increase the volume of your sales.

The more you put into your career, the more you will get out of it.

Like most jobs, success in sales is dependent on your drive, initiative, motivation and hard work.

Successful salespeople have several characteristics that set them apart from their colleagues.

The desire to sell

A successful salesperson has a desire to sell. If you want to be successful, focus on this single outcome. Direct everything you do towards making more sales. Strive to improve your selling techniques.

A successful sale involves selling solutions to people. People are interested in what the product can do for them. They are not concerned with all the specific features. Always concentrate on the benefits for the customer. Aim to satisfy customer needs and wants. You need to become a problem solver.

The desire to learn

A successful salesperson is always learning. Learning does not stop when you finish college or university. Continue to learn about your prospects, your customers, your products, your services, and your market. Learn more about how your company operates. Learn how to develop your sales techniques.

All markets continue to evolve. This leads to improvements in products, services and the methods of doing business. Continue to learn about these changes. Aim to become an expert in your chosen field.

Learn from other salespeople, such as work colleagues and your boss. Note what works with customers and what does not work. Attend seminars and study sales techniques books. Learn about those little incremental steps that lead to a big improvement in performance.

Strive to continue learning throughout your career. Never assume that you know it all. Keep an open mind. Study the developing techniques in your profession.

You can learn by experiencing, watching, listening, doing, discussing and studying. You can learn by reflecting daily on events and your performance.

Learn by asking the right questions and carefully considering the responses you receive. Learn by taking notes and reviewing them later. Learn by visualising. Learn by trial and error. Learn from your mistakes and failures. Learn by reviewing your behaviour. Learn by listening to advice and feedback. Learn from criticism received, constructive or otherwise.

If you want to succeed invest in yourself. The payback will be a successful career. Keep up to date with the latest developments.

The desire to connect

To succeed in sales you need to have an interest in people, first and foremost. Build networks of friends, associates, customers and others with a view to growing future business.

Change your perspective. You do not sell products to organizations. You sell benefits to unique individuals. Selling is all about people and relationships. You are selling to people who have emotions, fears, wants and desires.

People buy from people they like.

You need to connect emotionally with people to close a sale. Display empathy with customers in order to build rapport. Your priority is to become a friend who understands the concerns of his customers. It does not matter how good your company's products or services are. If you are to succeed then your customers must be willing to do business with you personally.

People buy from people whom they perceive to be like themselves.

Care for your customers and to strive to solve their problems. Your customers should feel that you are on their side. Talk to them about their hopes and desires. Identify mutual interests and talk about them.

Read business and current affair magazines and newspapers so that you can converse on topical issues.

Build trust in order to persuade and influence your customers. They need to feel that you are on their side. Help to solve their problems. Cater for their needs and wants.

People buy for their own reasons. Discover what these reasons are. Spend enough time with your customers to understand their needs and desires. Be honest and open with all of your customers.

Adapt your service to meet your customer's changing needs and desires. Provide the best service possible. Understand the importance of after service. Keep in contact with your customers even when you are not looking for orders.

The desire to make a difference

People buy from people they trust and respect. In most markets there is little to choose between the products of the main competitors. The professionalism, enthusiasm and performance of the salesperson involved is what wins the sale.

Go all out to make a difference to your customers. Provide a better service than your competitors. Ask your customers about their experiences with your service. Pass on any feedback you receive from customers. This will help to improve your company's products and services. Your continuous concern for your customers will lead to repeat sales.

You need to keep existing customers and increase the level of business with them. Make a difference to your customers and nourish the relationship with them.

The desire to qualify

To succeed in sales you need to find and acquire new customers. Work out how many prospects to approach each week in order to hit your sales targets.

Eliminate as soon as possible those prospects who cannot or will not buy your products. Make sure that you can spot the tyre kickers. Do not waste time if there is a low chance of converting a lead to sales. Instead concentrate on people who are more likely to buy your products.

If someone contacts you first, they are definitely interested. Make it a priority to identify their needs. This way you can emphasise those features of your product that meet their needs.

The easiest way to win is to get there first.

If a prospect contacts you after having spoken to a competitor, the sale will be much harder. The chances are that your competitor has already closed the sale. The prospect will just want a comparable quote. Be proactive in identifying and pursuing new prospects. Get there first if you want to succeed.

The desire to help

People prefer to buy rather than to be sold to. They do not want to be pressurised into making rash decisions. Aim to help customers by first finding out what they want and need. Then demonstrate those products that help to meet their needs. Be sincere in your desire to help customers. This will reap rewards through customer loyalty and repeat business.

Do not leave your customers with a feeling of buyer's remorse.

Understand how to meet a customer's needs and desires. Your customers should be satisfied with any deal that you strike. Always check that this is the case. Dissatisfied customers do not return for more.

Establish and nurture relationships with your customers. Your customers should want to buy your products. They should consider your service to be second to none. They should be happy to give you referrals. They should feel that they benefit from the relationship.

The desire to close

Your job is essentially about closing out sales. Prioritise everything else in order to maximise the number of closures. Closing is the ultimate goal.

Understand and employ several closing techniques to get the sale. This does not mean that you will trick or deceive your customers. Aim to establish a long-term relationship which will lead to repeat business.

You need to recognise and act on the buying signals.

Understand and pay close attention to body language. Recognise when people are ready to buy.

Buyers tend to be cautious. They look to avoid risk. Use this knowledge to help close the sale. Know when to apply a little more persuasion to close the sale. Know how to package the offering in order to close the sale. Know how to negotiate the right deal.

The desire to change

While the fundamental techniques of selling remain the same, you need to embrace change. Never be satisfied with your performance. Seek to improve it. Simply saying, "I have done my best" is not good enough. Always look for new ideas, concepts and methods.

Drop habits that are negative. They do not contribute to your goals. Work to improve your willpower and motivation levels. Learn new persuasion techniques. Study body language in order to understand your clients better. Improve your listening skills. Learn to build empathy. Increase your self-awareness.

Look for better ways to close sales. Look for better ways to service your customers.

The desire to be the best

Strive to be the best. Look to attract and retain customers. Customers should regard your total offering to be the best value for money around.

Set yourself apart from the competition.

Become the established expert on products, service and advice. Build a reputation for professionalism and integrity.

Organisation skills

Working in sales often feels like being self-employed. 90% of the time you may be away from the office. You need to use your own initiative. You need to be self-reliant. You need to be able to organise your working day and week. Discipline yourself to hit your own targets. You must learn to swim or sink.

At times the link from head office feels tenuous. You need to ensure their continuing support. Pay close attention to relationships with support staff. Cultivate these relationships. Always thank people when they help you out. Compliment them when you can.

Credibility and integrity

You need to establish credibility with the buyer in order to sell anything. Be open and honest with them. Tell the truth, even if it hurts. Never make exaggerated claims about your products that are not true. The customer will discover the truth eventually.

Integrity and honesty pay off in the long run. You can mention the disadvantages of your product without dwelling on them. This increases your credibility. The buyer will believe that you are being objective. This gives credibility to the rest of your sales pitch. You will build trust.

The main reason people refuse to buy is a lack of trust.

Customers rate trust as being the most important issue to them. Without credibility there cannot be trust. Without trust you will lose the business. Worse still you could lose other potential business. This will happen when the customer shares their bad experiences with others.

To be credible your actions must back up your words. If you make a promise you had better keep it.

There are times, because of circumstances beyond your control, when you cannot meet your promises. If this happens contact your customer immediately. Let them know the issue. Perhaps a delivery has been delayed due to a production problem. If you contact the customer immediately and explain the situation you will retain credibility. Perhaps you can offer to make a part delivery now and express deliver the balance when it is ready. The customer will be reassured that you are looking after their interests.

Listen to your customers. Build credibility into your presentations. Give examples of how you have helped other customers. Show potential customers testimonials from satisfied clients.

Self-confidence

To succeed you must have confidence and self-belief in your abilities. Once you believe you can win you will always find a way to succeed. Winning is all about belief, discipline and attitude. Ask any sports coach. They will tell you that most games are won and lost in the mind.

To be successful in sales you must begin by selling yourself.

Believe in yourself, your products, your services and the market opportunity. Whatever you are feeling, your customer will feel it also. Your customer will pick up on your emotions. If you do not believe in your products or services your customer will pick up on this. Remain positive in all encounters with your customers.

Self-discipline

You need self-discipline to succeed in sales. Make use of every single working day. Work harder than the opposition. Look to improve your working methods. Set targets and stick to them.

You will need to be thick-skinned. Learn not to take things personally. Get used to a certain amount of rejection. Salespeople have twice as many failures as they have successes. Get used to the idea.

A sense of humour

A sense of humour is a great help in a sales career. The ability to break the ice works wonders when talking to a new customer.

People buy from people they like. Try to develop a positive relaxed style spiced with a little humour and an optimistic outlook.

Chapter 2. The importance of proper communication

The ability to listen

The ability to listen is crucial in sales. If you do not listen properly you will not find out the customer's needs. You will also miss the customer's buying signals. Successful salespeople listen carefully to what their customers are saying.

Listening actively to your customers gives you a crucial advantage over the opposition.

Barriers to listening

Listening is the most important element of communication. Most people do not listen effectively. The average person only retains about 50% of what they hear. They are not actively listening. They do not receive the signals being sent to them.

There can be several reasons for this:

- They are not concentrating on the speaker.
- They are bored.
- They are preoccupied with their own thoughts or concerns.
- They are thinking about what they are going to say next.
- They do not understand the message.
- They are not interested in the message.

Barriers to receiving the message

Our senses can receive 11 million bits of information each second. However we can only process 40 bits of information per second. In addition our conscious mind can only store seven bits of information at any one time. If we tried to take everything in there would be instant overload.

We cope with these limits and avoid overload by ignoring most of the data that our senses receive. For instance we will concentrate on what is moving and ignore static objects. Our ears filter out repetitious background noise, such as a ticking clock. Instead they concentrate on loud or unusual noises which could signal danger.

We delete, distort or generalise most of the information received by our senses before we process it.

We concentrate on what we perceive to be important. It is the only way we can function. Bear this in mind when communicating with others. People do not always hear what you tell them. Even when they do, they often fail to retain the information.

We often fail to receive the message. There is effectively a barrier between us and the sender. The barrier may be caused by:

- Different interpretation of words or meaning.
- Hearing what we want to hear.
- Ignoring anything that conflicts with our beliefs or prejudices.
- Disliking the speaker.
- The message being sent through the wrong medium.
- Conflict between the speaker's words and body language.
- Overload – too much irrelevant information.
- Background noise.
- Distractions.
- Being emotionally or physically incapable of receiving the message.

When listening, give the speaker your complete attention. Do not multitask. Empty your mind of other concerns. Put aside all distractions. Concentrate solely on what the other person is saying.

Do not finish the other person's sentences. Do not hold prejudice. Keep an open mind. Do not think about what you are going to say next. Concentrate on understanding the message before you even think about responding.

Proactive listening

Most people think that listening is a passive skill. However effective listening is an active event. You can improve your listening skills by:

- Paying close attention to what is being said.
- Maintaining eye contact.
- Concentrating on the speaker, including his body language.
- Demonstrating by your own body language that you are paying attention.
- Smiling, nodding and making sounds of encouragement.
- Asking questions.
- Summarising and reflecting back what has been said.
- Mentally evaluating the message.

Proactive listening enables you to receive, interpret and understand the message. It enables you to understand the speaker's viewpoint and feelings.

By improving your listening skills you can build rapport with people. People will feel that you care about them. They will believe that you are interested in what they have to say. Proactive listening is vital when dealing with your team, superiors, clients, customers or suppliers.

You learn nothing while you are talking.

You learn most by listening and observing. Limit the time you spend speaking

Never interrupt

Never assume that you know what the customer is going to say. Do not interrupt. If you interrupt you do not receive the full message. Interrupting implies that you are not interested in what the speaker has to say. By implication you do not care about their problems and concerns. The customer will assume that you are only interested in making the sale. This leads to frustration on their part. It leads to lost sales opportunities.

Often people pause to collect their thoughts. They then continue with their conversation. Make sure that someone has finished their point before you respond.

Seek feedback and clarify the issues

Reflect and paraphrase the message. This will ensure that you have received it correctly. Ask questions to clarify the customer's point of view. Engage your brain before you engage your mouth.

Understand emotional signals

Study the customer's body language. Try to gauge your customer's emotional involvement. Listen out for the tone of voice. This indicates the importance to the customer of what is being said. Look for areas of concern. Concerns are usually broached first. Customers dwell on issues that concern them. If a customer repeats a topic, word or phrase, it is important to them.

What is implied is often more important than what is said.

Listen to what is being said. If the speaker is hinting at something, ask them to confirm the issue. Make sure that you interpret the message correctly.

Until you overcome concerns you cannot proceed. This applies to every stage of the sales cycle.

Mistakes to avoid when listening

There are several mistakes to avoid when listening:

- Interrupting the speaker.
- Changing the topic.
- Talking about your concerns.
- Well-intentioned comments.
- Criticising, advising, diagnosing, baiting.
- Concentrating on what you will say next.
- Pretending that you understand.
- Talking too much.
- Correcting the speaker.

Ask questions

People will begin a conversation for a specific reason. However they do not always get to the point. Perhaps they want to broach something but are unsure of the reaction they will get. Perhaps they have a problem with your product or service, but they are reluctant to mention it.

Listen carefully to what your customers say. Establish eye contact. Ask questions to elicit more information. Get them to open up. Ask them how they feel about issues. Probe them for further information. Eventually they will share their concerns.

Do not criticise, argue with or patronise your customers.

The ability to communicate

As well as the ability to listen, you need to develop the ability to communicate effectively. This involves knowing what to say, when to say it and how to say it. You need to respond appropriately. You need to be open, honest, respectful and thorough in your communication.

Recognise and overcome any existing barriers to communication.

Pay attention to body language

Pay attention to body language. Does the customer's body language back up what they are saying? If not, they may have some concern that they are reluctant to voice. Listen for signs of hesitancy or doubt. What is the underlying message? Think about why the customer has broached a topic. Ask them if there are any concerns. Encourage them to open up.

Look out for signs that people want to speak in group discussions. They may have a valid point that needs to be aired and discussed. Look for signs of confusion. You may need to clarify a point.

Listen out for what is implied.

Distinguish between facts and opinions

When someone is talking to you they will convey a mixture of facts and opinions. Make sure that you distinguish between the two. You must understand the difference between objective information and subjective beliefs.

You may want to take action based on the facts. However be wary of any proposed action based on opinions.

Your job as a salesperson involves persuading others and changing opinions.

Summarise

At the end of any conversation with a customer, summarise what has been agreed. Confirm the action to be taken and the time-line. You may have misinterpreted something. Summarising helps to confirm that you have received the message correctly.

Listening on the phone

It is even more important to pay close attention when listening on the phone. This is because you do not have the benefit of observing the speaker's body language.

Avoid using mobile phones if a landline is available. With mobile phones you have the added problem of poor signals.

Too many people talk on the phone while reading emails or searching through files. Do not make this mistake. Give the caller your undivided attention.

Multitasking does not work. You will inevitably miss an essential element of the conversation. You will have to ask the speaker to repeat himself. It will be blatantly obvious that you have not being paying attention. This sends the signal that you do not care about or respect the speaker.

Chapter 3. Setting Goals

To be successful you need to set goals. It does not matter where you start out. What matters is where you intend to end up and how you plan to get there.

Goals are a recognised and important aspect of a sales career. Salespeople and their employers are aware of the need to hit targets.

Pay structures reflect this through the payment of commission and bonuses. In addition prizes are periodically awarded to the best salespeople within a particular business.

Why Set Goals?

The advantage of setting goals is that they:

- Give you direction.
- Help to establish your priorities.
- Set a challenge for your team.
- Help you to keep score and monitor your progress
- Enable you to take corrective action and stay on track.
- Give you a sense of urgency and purpose.
- Help to uncover your potential.
- Provide a clear vision.
- Help you to stay motivated.
- Let you think ahead.
- Help to focus your mind.
- Create a sense of cohesion within your team.
- Ensure that you concentrate on important issues and drop other tasks.

Over 90% of people who take the time to set goals achieve their objectives.

Have a vision

To achieve success you first need an overall purpose to your life.

Align your long-term life goals to your personal values.

Write down your long-term life goals. Consider the person you want to be. Think about your unique skills and talents. Consider the qualities that you admire in others.

Your life goals should excite and inspire you. You should be passionate about your goals. Once you have an overall vision it will drive all of your future endeavours.

Long-term goals help you to grow and develop as a person.

Do not limit your vision

There is no limit to what you can achieve. You just need to adapt the right attitude.

You can reach any target you set for yourself.

If you believe in your abilities there is nothing that you cannot achieve. You just need to put in the effort. All things are possible.

You are surrounded by opportunities. Recognise them for what they are.

Most people see problems and obstacles. They are content to stop at them. Successful people see opportunities. They see learning steps which will take them to their desired destination.

Believe in yourself

The only limit to achieving your potential is your level of self-belief.

Self-limiting beliefs are the main factor in restricting your progress.

To succeed you must first believe that you can. You are in control of your own destiny. You are the person in charge. You control your own thinking. Believe in yourself.

You can choose to be positive and move forward. Alternatively you can choose to be negative and stall where you are. If you do not believe in yourself no one else will.

Winning requires a high degree of self-belief and discipline. Where there is a will, there is always a way. Believe in yourself and your products.

Your main function is to help people fulfil their wants and needs. If you believe that selling is manipulative then you will not have the will to succeed.

Set your overall career goals

Begin by setting your overall career goals. What do you want to achieve from your career? How much responsibility and accountability are you willing to accept? Think about the benefits that will accrue. Visualise yourself in the position. Imagine what it will be like.

Perhaps you want to become Vice President of Sales. Maybe you want to run your own business. Maybe you want to retire early. Write down exactly what you wish to achieve. Write down the benefits that will accrue with the role.

Success in life does not just happen.

Success comes about because we set goals. It happens because we make plans and commit to action. It occurs because we are prepared to overcome obstacles to get what we desire.

Set your own goals

Set your own long-term goals. Do not let others decide your long-term goals. You will only be motivated by your own long-term goals.

Your goals must reflect your values and beliefs.

Set medium term career goals

The next step is to take stock. Consider your current situation. Think about where you need to get to. Look at the intermittent steps that you need to take.

If your current job is Regional Salesperson then perhaps you first need to become Regional Sales Manager and then Regional Sales Director before becoming Vice President of Sales.

Take your first goal and set up a three-year plan to get there. Identify any extra training, qualifications and experience that you need to gain. Identify the goals that you need to meet in each area.

Subdivide each goal into further detailed steps.

So, for example, the need to gain experience can be subdivided further. You will need to learn more about prospecting, building rapport, identifying customer needs, pitching the sale, dealing with objections, closing the sale, negotiating and customer service. Aim to gain experience in each of these areas. Aim to improve your performance in all of them.

Schedule the steps required to reach each intermittent goal in turn.

Set short-term goals

For each individual area identify short-term goals. Thus for customer service you might decide to spend time in several departments to see how orders are received and processed.

So you might spend time in Purchasing, Accounts, Planning, Production, Quality Control, Shipping and Customer Services departments. You will learn how to prioritise orders. You will know how to chase up any problems that customers may have.

Set short-term goals for a window of no longer than three months.

Keeping a three-month plan instils a sense of urgency.

Prospecting goals can be to broken down to:

- Contact a given number of new prospects each week.
- Increase the ratio of prospects that agree to meet you.
- Increase the number of prospects that you can visit in a day.

Having set up your short-term goals you can then focus all of your attention on achieving them. Write out your short-term goals to ensure that you have not omitted anything. Prioritise and sequence the steps you need to take.

Writing down your goals is an essential first step to achieving them.

Writing down your goals allows you to set a time-line for the work. It helps you to focus on the necessary action.

By focusing on and meeting your short-term goals you will progress towards your medium term goals. At each stage keep your longer term goals in mind.

What happens without goals?

- Without goals you leave the result to chance.
- Without goals there is no vision.
- Without goals you waste time.
- Without goals you miss targets.
- Without goals you are destined for mediocrity.

People who do not set goals:

- End up working to other people's priorities.
- Become the followers in life.
- React to events rather than being proactive.
- Are busy, but not productive.
- Stagnate in their careers.
- Lack motivation.
- Achieve little of substance.

People who lack goals focus on issues to avoid, rather than on what they can achieve.

People who lack goals focus on problems and concerns. This leads to them becoming anxious and restless.

Have a reason

Have a clear reason for wanting to achieve your career goals. Money is not the main motivational driver. It is how you spend the money that will provide the motivation. This will give you impetus and keep you motivated.

Common reasons for setting long-term goals could be:

- To improve earnings.
- To increase savings.
- To buy a bigger house.
- To achieve status and recognition.
- To own a better car.
- Job satisfaction.
- To progress in your career.
- To achieve power and influence.
- Early retirement.
- To set up your own business.
- To buy a holiday home.

The personal benefits of achieving your professional goals must outweigh the cost involved.

Personal benefits > cost involved = success

When benefits exceed the cost involved you will gain long-term motivation. This is why it is important to write down the long-term benefits. Keeping these in mind will help you to overcome any obstacles you meet.

Share your goals

If you share your goals with others you will become more committed.

You will not want to lose face by not reaching your goals. You can share your goals with your spouse or your family. They can be a great source of encouragement when problems arise. So share your triumphs and your tribulations.

However the problem with family is that they care too much about you. They will accept the outcome if you do not reach your targets.

By also sharing your goals with a work colleague you are announcing that you will meet these goals. You will not want to look bad by giving in and having to admit failure. You will have additional motivation to succeed.

Set sales targets

Your annual sales targets will usually be set for you. Targets are normally linked to salary. Incentives such as commission or bonuses are paid for meeting and beating targets.

Convert your annual sales targets into monthly, weekly and daily targets.

So if you must sell 4600 widget each year then this converts to 100 each working week, assuming 6 weeks holidays. This equates to 20 widgets each working day for a five-day week. Therefore you must secure an average of 20 sales each day, *every day* to meet your annual target.

Set challenging targets

Set goals that are achievable but challenging. Include a degree of stretch in them. So if you need to achieve 20 sales each day to reach your bonus, why not set the daily target at 25? Imagine the benefits that you will accrue from beating the company target by 25%.

It is better to aim high and miss than aim low and hit.

Visualise the success. Think about the recognition and promotion success will bring. This will help to keep you motivated.

In sales your salary is directly linked to your performance. This is great news, because:

Your performance is solely under your control.

You are mostly left to your own devices. This means that you can put in as much effort as you like.

Daily targets

You need to hit your targets each and every day of the year. Selling is a daily task.

Each and every day counts. No day can be wasted.

Once a day is gone, it is gone. You cannot get it back. If you miss a daily target then you need to make it back before the end of the month. This concept is critical and transparent in sales.

Entrepreneurs who set up their own business often fail to understand the importance of setting daily sales targets. They are too consumed with the day-to-day running of their business. They forget that they need to hit daily sales targets to generate revenue and cash flow.

Daily priorities

Your number one daily priority is to hit your sales target. Prioritise any actions that enable you to do this

Everything else you do should be in support of this need to meet your sales. Delegate any less important tasks. Your priority is to get enough face-to-face meetings with prospects to convert them to the desired sales.

Weekly sales activity log

Keep a weekly sales activity log. This will help you to analyse your sales performance ratios. It will help you to manage your time better.

All of your targets and ratios should be specific and measurable.

You need to be able to measure your performance against all of your key targets and ratios. Measure your performance regularly. This enables you to control and manage it.

Keep a sales activity log.

Record the sales activities. Log the time, the duration, the activity, the customer, the result, the products sold and the revenue. Also log the customer's reason for buying in each case.

The sales activity log will show whether you have made the right number of cold calls, appointments and sales.

A weekly log also enables you to record details of any new prospects and referrals.

Personal mission statement

Consider preparing a personal mission statement. Focus this on your career, your values and ideals, your commitment to personal growth and your aspirations.

Make sure that you live up to your personal mission statement.

Consider displaying your mission statement at home or in the office as a source of inspiration.

Display your goals prominently

Revisit your goals daily. This will help to keep you motivated and on track. Display them prominently by your desk or on the wall as a reminder.

Perhaps you want to display and concentrate on a new goal or motivating phrase each day.

Focus on your performance

If you want to succeed focus on your performance. Focus on the tasks you need to carry out. Focus on the desired outcome. Focus on targets and what you need to do to achieve them.

Focus on what you can control or influence.

Focus your energy and activities where they will reap the most benefit.

Do not waste time worrying about issues that are beyond your control.

If an issue is beyond your control and influence, then it is someone else's job. Let them worry about it. You have enough on your own plate.

Become self-aware

Continually analyse your performance. Be aware of how you behave.

Your behaviour affects your results at every stage of the sales cycle.

Seek feedback from friends and colleagues. This will help you to become more self-aware. This in turn will lead to improved performance.

Celebrate success

Celebrate reaching milestones in your career. Perhaps you have won over a big contract or signed up a new important customer. Take time to celebrate this achievement with your work colleagues or your family. This will help to keep you motivated.

Recognising and acknowledging progress will help to keep you and your team motivated.

Celebrate in proportion to the achievement. Involve everyone who helped you to make that achievement.

Life is more about the journey than the destination.

Take time to enjoy the little things that matter. Celebrate reaching each milestone. Celebrate with family and friends.

Even when you are doing well you need to be planning for future success.

Stick to the path

Having set your goals, keep working towards them. You must remain proactive.

Take full advantage of each day.

Meeting your long-term goals is not a sprint activity. It is more akin to a journey, with staging points along the way.

Be consistent in your approach. Maintain impetus by taking incremental daily steps in the right direction. Stay on course.

You will face your fair share of setbacks and obstacles along the way. The important thing is to remain positive. Focus on your goals. Stick to the path. Do not stray. Do not falter.

Accept the cost

Little of value in this life comes easy. To achieve success you must work for it. If you want to be the best you will need to make certain sacrifices.

Drop negative habits that are debilitating.

Focus instead on actions that yield results. If you need to study ten hours each week to pass an exam, then watch less television.

Accept responsibility

You are responsible for your own actions. You are accountable. You are culpable.

Do not shift the blame elsewhere.

When things go wrong do not blame colleagues, your boss, your products or your customers. Do not blame the competition, the economy, the exchange rate, the weather or anything else.

The buck stops with you. Do not make excuses. Do not whine.

Take stock and learn from your setbacks. Focus on solutions, not the problems.

Chapter 4. Time management

Advantages of managing your time

Everyone has the same available time each day. You can achieve more by working longer and working harder than everyone else. However there is a limit to the available hours. There is also a danger from stress or burn out.

The best way to maximise your achievements is to manage your time effectively and efficiently.

Aim to achieve more in less time than others.

Effective time management can:

- Simplify your life.
- Reduce stress levels.
- Increase your effectiveness.
- Increase your efficiency.
- Increase your job satisfaction.
- Increase your productivity.
- Improve your work-life balance.
- Help further your career.

Maximise customer contact time

To succeed in sales manage your time. Prioritise your workload. Concentrate on the important tasks that lead to sales. Balance conflicting priorities.

The solution is to do the most productive thing possible at any given time.

Aim to maximise customer contact time. Customer contact time generates sales. You will not generate sales through small talk with colleagues. It is the conversations with customers that pay off.

Time spent with customers is paramount.

Understand the difference between activity and achievement.

Being busy is not the same as being productive.

As well as working harder you must learn to work smarter. Focus on the areas where you have real control or influence. Focus on what you can change for the better. It is futile to waste time worrying about issues that are beyond your sphere of influence.

Prioritise your work

The best way to plan your work is to create to do lists each evening. Then prioritise your work for the next day. Cross out each task as you complete it. This will help to keep you motivated.

Drop tasks that are neither important nor urgent.

Recognise distractions for what they are.

Delegate as much as you can. This frees you up to concentrate on the important issues.

Aim to find balance in your life. Make time for family and friends. Get a hobby. Become more efficient in what you do. Time management techniques help you to become more efficient and effective.

Plan your territory

Subdivide your territory. Plan and group your visits to make the best use of your time. Combine visits to cut down on travelling time.

Time management tips

- Set realistic short-term targets.
- Keep a to do list.
- Plan each day the evening before.
- Utilise marginal time such as travelling time.
- Develop a routine and stick to it.
- Plan and schedule your work in advance.
- Be productive, not busy.
- Break old negative habits.
- Use tools such as a diary, wall planner, personal organiser and calendars.
- Keep one diary for all your plans, schedules, meetings and appointments.
- Set time limits on tasks.
- Target to be early.
- Break larger tasks down into smaller, more manageable tasks.
- Delegate as much as you can.
- Remain proactive rather than reactive.
- Make timely decisions.
- Avoid procrastination.
- Handle paperwork and emails only once.
- Categorise and file your emails and paperwork.
- Remove yourself from unwanted circulation lists.
- De-clutter your desk and office.
- Manage your boundaries.
- Manage meetings effectively.
- Bin irrelevant information.
- Keep and review activity logs.
- Learn to say no.
- Look at better ways of doing things.

Chapter 5. Why people buy

Understand why people buy from you

Record the reasons customers buy from you. Eventually you will get to know the top 5 or 6 reasons for buying. Incorporate this knowledge into your sales proposals.

The purchase cycle

The typical customer goes through several stages in a purchase cycle:

- The customer becomes or is made aware of the product.
- The customer develops an interest in the product before deciding to evaluate it.
- The customer develops a desire for the product, which leads to the decision to buy.

You need to make people aware of your products. Help them to develop an interest in your offering. Get them onto the purchase cycle and move them through the stages.

Wants and needs

People may buy from you for many reasons.

> ***People buy either because they want something or they need something.***

People also buy if the product will prevent something undesirable happening to them.

> ***Businesspeople buy results.***

In a business environment people buy because they want to change something. They may want to make a process improvement. Perhaps they want a better quality product. Perhaps they want to reduce costs.

Benefits

People do not buy products because of their features. They buy the benefits that these features bring.

> *People buy those benefits that meet their individual needs.*

People buy products that bring a positive impact. The products need to represent value for money. The motive for buying must outweigh the option of doing nothing. Before deciding to buy the customer evaluates if the product can help them now and in the future.

> *In a business environment the buyer concentrates on satisfying needs.*

Individual customers in a retail environment are more concerned with satisfying wants rather than needs. Most retail products are not what we would classify as essentials, such as food, shelter or clothing.

> *Perceived value > price = sale*

In each transaction the perceived value to the customer must outweigh the price in order to convince him to buy the product.

Consequences

For every purchase the buyer weighs up the risk of buying against the consequences of not buying.

Make the customer *feel* that they will experience pleasure and satisfaction from the product. When people anticipate the benefits they will be motivated to buy the product.

When the customer *feels* that they can avoid the pain of not buying they will be motivated to avoid this negative experience.

Of the two influencing factors avoiding the pain is always the greater motivator. This knowledge is applied in many closing techniques.

Who people buy from

Selling is a personal experience. People buy from people, but not just any people.

People buy from people that they like.

- People buy from people they trust.
- People buy from people in whom they have confidence.
- People buy from people who they think are like themselves.
- People buy from people who take the time to understand their needs and concerns.
- People buy from people with market knowledge who give them the right product advice.

Therefore you need to build rapport with customers. Build friendships that last.

People buy for emotional reasons rather than logical reasons.

Reassure your customers that they are making the right choice when deciding to buy. Tell them that you will look after their business personally. You will make sure they get the best possible service.

Strive to add value to your customers in every encounter. If you assist customers they will return for more. They will also recommend you to others.

Emotional reasons for buying

End consumers often buy for emotional rather than logical reasons. Below are some examples of emotional reasons for buying:

- To feel secure.
- To avoid pain or loss.
- To be recognised.
- To achieve status.
- To achieve power.
- To belong to a group.
- To give something back to society.
- To make someone else feel good.
- To make themselves feel good.
- To impress their superiors.
- To feel attractive.
- To be liked.
- To feel loved.
- To have fun.
- To simplify their life.
- To reduce stress.
- To learn something.
- To improve their health.
- To feel important.
- To enhance their ego.
- To keep up with their neighbours.

Logical reasons for buying

Business people usually buy for logical reasons. Some logical reasons for buying are:

- To fulfil a need, either real or imagined.

- To solve a problem they are experiencing.
- To improve productivity.
- To improve performance.
- To improve reliability.
- To get better delivery.
- Convenience.
- To reduce costs.
- To avoid or reduce risk.
- To gain a competitive edge.

Issues that will interest the buyer

A number of issues will interest the buyer:

- The products and services you offer.
- How the product meets their needs or wants.
- Any guarantees or warranties.
- The reputation of your company.
- Your experience and that of your company.
- Your unique selling point.
- Your prices.
- Your discounts or offers.
- The timing of the proposal.

Explain these issues in any presentation you give.

Buyer concerns

A typical buyer has several concerns, including:

- Am I being asked to pay too much?
- Do I have enough information to make the buying decision?
- Will I miss my procurement targets?
- What are the consequences if I make the wrong decision?
- Can I handle the change involved?
- Can I trust the salesperson?
- Will I look good or bad as a result of the deal?

- Can I justify the purchase to myself and colleagues?
- What after sales support can I get?
- What are the consequences of not buying the product?
- Is it safer not to proceed at this stage?

Chapter 6. The sales cycle

The sales cycle is represented in Figure 1 below. There are seven stages to the traditional sales cycle, which ends with the closing of the sale. In the example below I have added two additional stages. These stages emphasise the importance of repeat business.

At any time different prospects will be at different stages of the sales cycle.

You need to work at each of the stages to hit your sales targets.

All stages of the sales cycle are equally important and each stage needs attention.

If you are dealing with a client at any particular stage, aim to move them to the next stage.

Aim to build commitment incrementally.

If you cannot move a customer to the next stage log the reason and issues. Come back to the customer after a couple of months. Concentrate meanwhile on other more promising prospects.

If you avoid any stages of the sales cycle you will not succeed.

Many salespeople find prospecting a difficult stage.

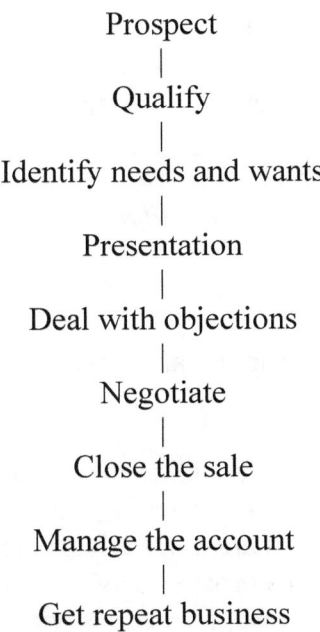

Figure 1 The sales cycle

The funnel

The sales funnel is a pipeline full of suspects, prospects and customers at each stage of the sales cycle. The funnel is widest at the opening where new suspects are gathered. Prospects drop out at every stage of the sales cycle. The funnel gets narrower as this happens.

> ***Gather as many prospects into your sales funnel as possible.***

Work out your conversion rate at each stage of the sales cycle. Work out the value of your average order. Look at your sales targets. Now work backwards and calculate how many new prospects you need to gather each week. The more you gather, the greater your success will be.

Analyse your conversion rates

Analyse your conversion rates at each stage of the sales cycle.

Compare your conversion rates with other salespeople in your organization.

Aim to be the best at each stage.

If your score is low in a particular area review your methods in that area.

Talk to the salespeople who do well in this particular area. Accompany them when they are carrying out this activity. Look at what they are doing that you are not. Perhaps they omit something that you include which turns prospects away. Perhaps you are saying the wrong things. Perhaps you are saying the right things at the wrong time.

Expect resistance at every stage

Expect prospects to resist your proposals at every stage. Be prepared to persevere in order to succeed.

You will hear the word 'No' about seven times before you get to the close.

You may have to revisit the customer at least seven times before you get to the close. Do not give up. Do not accept 'No' as a final answer at any stage. If you do the business will go to someone else.

The customer will buy

If you do the right things at each stage of the sales cycle the customer will want to buy. You will not need to push the sale. Just lead the customer to the point where they feel willing and comfortable to commit to your products.

To get a sale you must first get a prospect's attention. Then develop an interest and desire in your product. Only then can you close the sale.

The customer will demand a minimum level of service

Today's customers are more discerning. They have developed higher expectations.

Customers expect a quality product with excellent service levels.

Customers expect immediate, convenient, tailored individualized levels of service. You will not retain customers if you do not meet these expectations.

Chapter 7. Finding new business

Differentiating prospects from suspects

You cannot close every sale. A given percentage of people will not buy no matter how well you perform. With experience you will increase the ratio of closures. However you cannot convert every opportunity into a sale. There will always be a need to find new business to replace lost sales.

To maximise sales you need to get more appointments. To get more appointments you need to find more prospects.

Until you have confirmed a prospect they remain a suspect.

A suspect is a brand-new lead. One that you have identified but not yet contacted.

To identify if a suspect is a prospect ask the following questions:

- Have they got a problem that your product can solve?
- Do they need your product, whether they realise it or not?
- Can you create a desire in them to own your product?
- Do they have the finances to buy the product?
- Have they got the authority to make the buying decision?

If all of these conditions are present then your suspect becomes a prospect.

Prospects deserve your immediate undivided attention. Find out if they are willing to buy. Contact them and arrange to meet them.

Having identified prospects you should target and develop them. You then need to qualify your prospects. Drop prospects who are unlikely to buy. However do not prejudge anyone based on their appearance, their clothing or their speech.

Establish your customer profile

Identify your customer profile. This will help you to attract new prospects: Understand:

- Who is likely to buy your products?
- Why do people buy your products?
- Where are potential buyers likely to be located?
- How can you identify likely buyers?

The answers to these questions will help you to build a customer profile. Seek out people who match this profile. They are the most likely group to buy your products. Contact sufficient prospects each week to generate the required sales.

Real success lies in the quality of your leads.

You need a set of qualifying criteria to obtain quality leads. Do not waste time on people who cannot or will not buy from you.

Rejecting unsuitable suspects

Reject unsuitable suspects at an early stage.

Discard anyone for whom you cannot provide a service.

If your products do not meet a customer's needs then do not waste any further effort.

Also reject anyone who cannot afford the product. Before doing this consider if you can arrange financing.

You can always return to a customer if their circumstances improve.

Your initial contact may not have the authority to place an order. In this case get the details of the decision maker. Arrange to contact this person as soon as possible.

The importance of prospecting

Continually look for qualified leads. Your aim is to find new potential customers. Without prospects you cannot find new sales.

Prospecting is the most important aspect to sales success.

Getting new prospects needs to be an integral and daily part of your routine.

If you can double the number of new prospects you meet you can double your sales.

Without new prospects you are going to fail. It is the starting point. It is the first step on the road to success.

Every time you make a sale think about the number of new prospects you must contact to replace that sale.

Fear of prospecting

Many salespeople dread prospecting. They fear rejection. They dislike and feel uncomfortable making that initial contact. They lack confidence and self-belief.

When you approach any new prospect their initial reaction is usually one of cautious negativity.

Overcome this natural human reaction by building rapport as soon as possible.

This initial negative reaction makes many salespeople apprehensive. This leads to procrastination by the salesperson. They avoid the task. This results in lost sales and missed targets.

Adapting the right attitude

To succeed in prospecting you need to adapt a positive attitude. Accept that rejection is a natural part of the process.

> ***This rejection is not a reflection on your self-worth.***

The customer is rejecting the product, not you as a person.

Set targets

Set yourself a target to find enough new prospects each week. Then take the necessary action to meet this target. Your target should be results driven. Perhaps you want to meet five new prospects each day.

Keep your eyes and ears open for new business.

> ***Look for referrals through all of your contacts and existing customers.***

Set yourself a target of *converting* a given number of prospects each week.

> ***You must continue to prospect even when sales are good.***

Setting clear targets helps to keep you focused and on track. Remain positive and enthusiastic when dealing with prospects. Believe in yourself and your abilities. The customer will detect any negativity. This will lead to rejection and failure.

Strike when the iron is hot

When you get a new prospect act promptly. If someone is interested in buying then move quickly. The prospect may act on their own initiative and buy a competitor's product. Maybe a competitor will get to them first. Either way you could lose the sale.

The salesperson who makes contact first usually gets the business.

Chapter 8. The nature of your customer base

Regardless of your business type, your customer base can usually be subdivided into the following groups:

- Customers who regularly buy your products.
- Seasonal customers who buy at one time of year.
- Customers who have made one off buys.
- Potential customers who are aware of your company or products.
- Potential customers who have not heard of your company or products.

You can generate extra business from all of these categories. Make sure that you target all of these categories.

How to get extra business from regular customers

There are two ways to get extra business from regular customers:

- Increase the frequency of their purchases.
- Increase their average order size.

Your current customer base is your richest seam of potential business.

Keep in regular contact with existing customers. Let them know about special promotions, bulk buy offers, upcoming sales, promotional events or exhibitions. Give them special offers for being valued customers.

Find out which additional products your existing regular customers would be interested in. Find out why they do not buy certain products. Perhaps you can alter the offering to entice them to buy these products.

Develop your product range to suit the stated needs of your largest and most loyal customers.

Ask your regular customers about other departments and branches within their organizations. Get a referral to help you to set up a meeting with the relevant buyer.

Know the life cycle of your product.

Most customers who buy a new car will consider changing it two and a half years after purchase. They will probably change before three years are up.

In this case you would return to existing customers just when they are thinking about replacing their car. Ask them how they enjoyed their current car. Find out what is important to them. Perhaps their circumstances have changed and they now need an estate version. Let them know about the benefits of the new model range. Invite them for a test-drive. Sell them on the technical advances.

If the average household owns 2.5 cars then why stop when you have sold one car?

If you sell to the husband, ask about the wife and the teenage children. Find out what model they are driving now. Ask how long they have owned it and how often they change cars. Get their contact details. Make contact when the time is right.

How to get extra business from seasonal customers

Talk to your seasonal customers. Meet up with them.

Find out why your seasonal customers only buy your products at certain times.

Show them your complete product range. Perhaps there are other products that they might buy. Perhaps they buy at one time of the year to take advantage of special promotions. Consider how you can offer them discount at other times of the year. You could do this if they agree to buy a given volume.

Keep in contact with seasonal customers all year round.

This will show that you are genuinely interested in them. Perhaps you could sign them up on an annual contract. This will commit them to your company.

How to get extra business from customers who made a one-off purchase

Ring up customers who have made a one-off purchase. Tell them that you value their business. Ask about their experience.

Find out if there was a problem for one-off customers.

Many customers do not return if their initial experience is bad. They turn their back and simply walk away. Ask one-off customers if there was a problem with the service that they received. Tell them that you want to ensure that all customers get an excellent level of service.

If there was a problem, then find out the details. If the service was poor then offer them discount for repeat business. Assure them that you will personally ensure that the level of service is excellent.

Perhaps they were not satisfied with the product. In this case show them your wider product range. Ask for a meeting to demonstrate your products.

One-off customers can be converted to seasonal or regular customers.

All you need to do is rectify the issue for them. Then pay attention to their individual needs.

Reactivating previous customers

Visit prior customers.

Find out why previous customers no longer buy from your company.

Have these customers gone to a competitor? What was the reason? Did their needs change? Perhaps your products have since developed to meet their existing needs.

It is easier to reactivate previous customers than it is to find new customers.

You already have a previous relationship with old customers. There is a degree of existing trust. Offer them special introductory terms. Let them know about current sales or promotions.

Look at the records of salespeople who have left your organisation

Every firm has turnover of staff. Get hold of the client list and records of any salespeople who have left your firm. There will be an abundance of qualified leads in this list. Re-establish contact with these people.

Do not simply phone these people or send a letter. Go and visit them.

Getting extra business from potential customers who are aware of your company

This group includes:

- People targeted by your marketing team
- People who have turned down business in the past.
- People who have made a past enquiry.
- People to whom you have given your business card.

Target this group regularly. They are your biggest source of new prospects. Try to build relationships. Eventually these leads will convert to sales. At the very least you may get a referral.

How to sell more to existing customers

Try some of the following to get extra sales:

- Sell more products or services.
- Sell the latest model, upgrade or improvement.
- Sell to other branches of their business.
- Sell to other departments within their business.
- Provide seasonal offerings.
- Offer special promotions.
- Provide valued customer offerings.

Multiple contacts

Have several contacts for each customer. Remember that you sell to people.

The problem with buyers is that they have a tendency to retire, move to other jobs or die.

Have more than one contact with each customer. You must not lose the business if a buyer moves on.

If a buyer is moving jobs, then get him to introduce you to his replacement. This will enable you to build a relationship with the new buyer.

Always keep in contact with buyers when they move jobs. Ring them up. Check out the possibility of you doing business with their new employer.

Online search engines

You can use online search engines to find out about new prospects. Check out company web sites. Do this before making your first contact.

You can also use search engines to find new prospects. Look out for membership of societies, special interest groups or professional institutions.

Ring the switchboard

You may come across a new company that is likely to do business with you. If you cannot find a suitable contact from their web site just ring up and ask. Just give your name and your company name. Then ask for the details you need.

If you fail to get the information from the switchboard operator, just ask for the Customer Services department. They will probably give you the details that you need.

Chapter 9. Obtaining referrals

Referrals

The easiest way to get new prospects is through referral from others.

> *It is easier and quicker to close a referred lead.*

You can work two referred leads in the time it takes to work one non referred lead.

> *The more referrals you get the more successful you will be.*

Prospecting is not easy. Building that initial rapport can be difficult. People are defensive when approached by an unknown salesperson.

Mentioning a friend or colleague buys you a few minutes to establish interest. Referrals help you to build trust.

> *Every customer has a circle of influence that you can tap into.*

Referrals are an excellent way of getting new prospects. Having sold to one person you can also sell to their friends and acquaintances. If your friend gets a new car, the chances are that you want one too. Peoples' friends are likely to be in the same financial bracket. They will be able to afford your products.

> *Build trust before you ask for a referral.*

Recognise the potential

Recognise the potential in every encounter. You may not get what you set out to achieve. However you need not leave empty-handed.

Nurture every relationship.

Customers who do not buy today may buy in three months time. A business that is too small to service today may grow into a valuable customer in the future. A buyer who rejects your current product range may like the products currently under development.

Just because a prospect turns you down, it does not mean that they cannot give you a referral.

Grow the seeds today to reap the harvest later.

Referral after refusal

A prospect may refuse to place an order. If this happens ask them for a referral.

Most people will offer a referral in this situation. Human nature dictates that they will want to make up for refusing the sale.

Referrals from existing customers

The best place to get referrals is from existing customers.

Ask for referrals from all existing customers.

Pick the right moment when asking for the referral.

Perhaps you have helped a customer to replenish their stock by delivering early on an order. If so, then this is the perfect time to ask for a referral. The customer will feel obligated to return the favour.

Referral after closing

If you close a sale ask for a referral to another customer.

If you have reduced the price or added some extras, the customer will feel obliged to reciprocate.

Referral after first delivery

If a new customer has just received his first delivery and is pleased with your product it is an excellent time to ask for referrals.

Referrals from other salespeople

Get referrals from other salespeople who sell complementary products. Offer to swap referrals with them. Perhaps you are selling computer hardware and someone else is selling software. If you refer each other and pass on prospect details, you will both gain from the arrangement.

Ask your current customers for the contact details of people selling them complementary products. Then contact these salespeople and propose to swap referrals.

You can even make an arrangement with salespeople for similar products.

Perhaps one of your prospects wants a feature that your product lacks and you cannot close the sale. You know that your competitor's product has this feature. You therefore refer this prospect to the other salesperson. In return he does the same for you with prospects that he cannot close.

Discuss swapping referrals with salespeople you meet at sales conventions or exhibitions.

Referrals from your service department

If you sell mechanical, electrical or computer equipment then your firm probably has a service department.

Regularly check with your service department to see who has been calling for repair work. Once the equipment begins to break down people start to think about the possibility of replacing it. So check with your service department for potential leads.

Questions to elicit referrals

Apply the correct technique to elicit referrals.

Do not simply ask a current customer if they know anyone who might need the product.

They usually respond with, "I cannot think of anyone right now, I will get back to you." Their mind goes blank. You are asking them to select one person from hundreds of people they know.

Narrow the choice for them.

Narrow the choice by asking if they are a member of a club, a society or similar organization. Then ask them to refer you to a fellow member of their club. The customer may not be a member of any clubs. If so ask about his close friends.

This technique engages the customer at an emotional level. It is more likely to produce results.

In an office environment when asking for referrals you could glance at a customer's computer. The buyer will realise the information he needs is stored there.

Get all the names first.

If the customer begins to give you a name just smile and nod. Do not jot it down immediately. Ask for a second name. He is likely to have more than one. Jot down all the names he gives you. When he has finished go back to the first name you jotted down. Get all the contact details for this person. Repeat this for all the names he has given you.

Ask for his permission to use his name when approaching these prospects. Ask who you should approach first. This will be the best lead.

Return for more referrals

If you get several referrals from clients, they will probably be able to give you more.

Tell them how the previous referrals worked out. There will be other contacts that they have remembered meanwhile. They will be happy to pass on these details when you ask for them.

Include a section in your sales form

Include a section for referral details in your sales form. Then just ask for the information when you are collecting the other sales data.

References

You can ask an established customer to act as a reference. Once they agree you give their contact details to new prospects. These prospects can then contact the existing customer directly. They are free to ask the existing customer about their experience. They will inevitably ask about your service levels and their thoughts on your products.

Offer incentives to customers who provide references.

It is standard procedure to offer extra incentives to customers who are willing to provide a reference. A conservatory manufacturer may offer a 15% discount to customers willing to allow 10 new prospects to contact them directly.

Make sure that all reference customers receive a first-class service from you.

Advertising in the trade press

If you place an advert in the trade press your target audience will probably read it.

Anyone responding to trade advertisements will be qualified leads.

Direct mailing

Carefully research the target list before issuing direct mail. Send the promotional material to a named individual, marked 'Private and confidential.' This way the target person will open the envelope and scan the material.

Send a letter with your brochure to summarise the benefits of your offering. Target the benefits to the company and the individual. Keep the letter short. Three short paragraphs are enough. End the letter by saying that you will ring after a week to briefly discuss what you can offer.

Always follow up direct mail campaigns with phone calls.

You must be proactive and take the initiative.

Begin your benefits letter with a benefits question. Choose a question which will prompt the reader to continue reading. Write something like the following in bold writing at the top:

"Want to save 30% on your heating bills? Call Peter Smith on 01485 333333"

Family and friends

If your products are good enough for everyone else why not sell them to family and friends? Do this in a manner that will not alienate them. You do not want your friends to avoid you because they are embarrassed to refuse to buy from you.

Just tell them which products are available. Tell them that you would be delighted to supply their needs. Then tell them that you will not be mentioning the products again when you next meet. It is up to them to ask you. You do not want them to buy because they are your friends. You want them to buy because the products meet their needs.

This removes any pressure. Your friends will be relaxed about the situation.

Related industries

Related industries are a good source of prospects. Perhaps you are selling office equipment and someone else is maintaining it. They can let you know which businesses have the oldest equipment. They may know who may be looking to upgrade their equipment soon.

In return you can recommend them for the maintenance contract when you make a sale.

Trade shows

Attend industry events, trade shows and exhibitions. Ideally your company will provide a stand at one of these events. It is a great way to find new customers. It also helps to strengthen contacts with existing customers.

Professional bodies

Join professional bodies or trade associations. They are a great place to network.

Demonstrations – free trial giveaways

Get your product in front of potential customers. Select somewhere where footfall is high.

Open Days

Invite prospective customers to your premises. Include special offers for loyal and new customers.

Networking

Attend exhibitions, business presentations and events in order to meet potential customer.

Read business papers and journals to find out about upcoming events. Check the local chamber of commerce or round table for their schedule of events.

If you attend an event with a colleague split up. Do not waste time socialising with each other. Split up and work the room.

Networking enables you to convert business contacts to new customers. Networking enables you to exchange business cards. You can gather contacts and follow up on them later.

Aim to spend about five hours each week networking in the evenings.

Work out where your potential customers network. Join the right clubs or associations. Have a target list of the people you want to contact. Maintain momentum every week. Keep a positive attitude and have fun.

Sales lead

A sales lead may come from someone else within our company. Customer services will often receive calls from prospective clients. They can pass the details onto the salesperson for that region.

These leads will result in sales as the client has made the first contact and is obviously interested.

You may get a sales lead from existing customers. They may give you the contact details of buyers from different regions of their company.

Chapter 10. Establishing contact

Advertising and marketing are both one-way processes aimed at generating interest and a response.

The real business of selling only begins when you establish contact and have a two-way conversation.

Your opening is just as important as your closing.

Your opening shot needs to be good. You need to establish credibility by appearing and sounding professional. You also need to grab the prospect's attention and stimulate interest.

If you don't open well the customer will not be around for the closing.

Start at the top

Contact the senior decision maker first. This person will usually refer you to someone lower in the organization. However you will have registered your intent. You can then keep them updated on your progress. Also you will gain access to the person that they refer you to.

Senior people expect you to get to the point immediately. Concentrate your opening on the savings you can bring to their organization.

If you begin at middle management level you will not be referred up the chain of command. People will use their power to stall and block you. This occurs because of various internal political reasons.

Know your target

Research your target before you make contact. Find out about their leadership style. How do they like to get things done?

Find out about their business. Research their likely needs and how your product can help them. Think about those features of your products which can add the most benefit to them.

Anticipate the most likely objections and how you will answer them.

Any personal information you gather in advance will help you to build rapport.

Practise your pitch

Practise your pitch with your boss or other company salespeople.

The more you practise the better you will get.

The product offer

Produce a clear, concise, product offer. Summarise:

- The unique perceived benefits.
- The main features and their advantages.
- Any proposed promotion.

The product offer is used to promote the offering to potential customers.

Include the product offer in sales brochures and marketing material. Include the product offer on your website. Use the product offering as part of scripted notes for cold calling.

First contact

Emotionally engage the prospect with your opening pitch. Use it to set yourself apart from the competition.

Think about the benefits you bring to people. Express this in a few short sentences. Think of something distinctive about your product or service. Express this in a novel way designed to prompt the prospect to ask for more information.

When you first contact a prospect immediately get several points over. Within the first minute they should understand that:

- Your visit or call will be short.
- You have a new service or product that can meet their needs.
- There are no obligations.
- There will be no pressure.

Quickly establish that you are talking to the right person, with the authority to buy. If there are other decision makers get their details. Try to get a face-to-face meeting. This is the best way to build rapport. This will enable you to find out all the needs and possible objections.

Timing

People are busy. They are not readily accessible. There are many competing distractions for their time and attention.

Do not call at an inconvenient time.

It is best to call new prospects in the morning. Do not phone first thing, when people catch up on emails and correspondence.

Do not ring on a Monday morning, when most people plan their diaries for the week.

If someone tells you the time is not convenient do not persist with the call. You will not have their undivided attention. Instead ask for a convenient time to ring back.

Telephoning new prospects

The first contact with a new prospect is daunting for many salespeople. Try to meet face-to-face, rather than phoning them up. Never make first contact by email.

> *Create a basic script of what you want to cover.*

Use a checklist to ensure that you have gathered all the relevant information. Think about the likely objections. Work out how you will answer these objections.

> *You only have about 15 seconds to attract attention.*

If you have a referral you are more likely to get a few minutes to make your pitch.

> *People do not like to receive unsolicited calls. Their natural reaction is to be defensive.*

Do not aim to sell anything over the phone. Aim to get a face-to-face meeting. This will give more time to read body language and build rapport.

Your cold calling technique will improve with practice and experience. Just make sure that you make enough calls to meet your targets. Develop a habit of contacting a given number of people each day. You can overcome anxiety by developing a plan. Know in advance what your objective is. This may be to:

- Qualify that you have a prospect.
- Get referrals if they are not a suitable prospect.
- Make an appointment to demonstrate your products.
- Get permission to deal with a subordinate.

Ring in person. Do not get a secretary to make the call and put you through. Speak a little slower than normal. Use emphasis and inflection to help make your points.

Introduce yourself. Qualify that the contact has the authority to buy your products. If not get the contact details of the correct person. Give the name of anyone who has referred you. Mention anyone else you already know from their company. Mention any common acquaintances.

Get to the point quickly. Smile and relax. Be friendly, polite and enthusiastic. Stand up when making these calls. It makes you sound more decisive. Reassure the prospect that you will only take a few minutes of their time.

Never try to sell anything over the phone on a first call.

It is difficult to sell anything over the phone. You are a stranger who is making an unsolicited call. There is no basis for trust. Ask for a twenty minute face-to-face meeting. If you ask for an hour you are unlikely to get it.

Mention your products or services. If they use a similar product or service, ask them about it. Ask what they like about the product. This is less threatening than asking what they do not like. It will let you know what is important to them.

Never ask a negative question.

Always rephrase negative questions to turn them into positive questions. Never ask what a customer does not like. Instead ask which extra features they would like or which improvements would be important to them.

Having found out what is important to the prospect you can then mention your offering. Concentrate on those benefits that they currently lack.

Be tactful in your approach. Never imply that the customer made a poor purchase decision with their current product. If you do this they will drop you like a hot potato. Praise their current choice. Say that it was a logical buy at the time. However point out that technology has moved on. Then mention the relevant extra benefits of your product range. Ask for an appointment to demonstrate your products.

Concentrate on the needs of their company and how you can meet them.

Limit the time spent talking about you and your company. Instead mention the savings you managed to bring to their competitors. This helps to build credibility. If you have sold to a prestigious company in their industry then mention this.

Once you get the first meeting you can find out the prospect's needs. You can build rapport. You can arrange a second meeting to present your product offering.

Follow up the phone call with an email, confirming the date and time of the scheduled meeting.

Cold call example

People who receive unsolicited calls switch off quickly. Get to the point immediately. Ask an open-ended question to get the response you want. An example would be:

"Good morning John, my name is Peter Jones from Diamond Handling Systems. For the last year we have been working with Midlands Assembly and have managed to help them significantly reduce their operational assembly costs. Tell me John, how important is operational efficiency to you?"

You can make the opening pitch using three sentences.

- The first sentence introduces you and your company.
- The second sentence establishes your credibility and gives a reference that can be checked.
- The third sentence is an open question designed to lead the prospect in the direction you want.

Your reference should be from a well-known prestigious client. Describe the nature and extent of the benefit that you have brought to this client. The client will obviously answer that efficiency and cost saving are important. Respond by quantifying the savings you can bring. Then ask for a ten minute meeting to find out the prospect's needs.

Cold call response

You are likely to get several different responses to your opening pitch. You should handle these in different ways.

The prospect may ask what it is that you are selling. Take this as a buying signal. Continue with your pitch. Briefly explain your offering and the benefits to the prospect.

They may say that savings are obviously important to them. If so continue with the pitch.

They may say that they are too busy. If so arrange a time to call back.

The prospect may say that they have just improved their systems. This is an objection. Ask about the single most important problem facing them now. You may uncover a problem where your products or services can be of benefit.

If the prospect tells you that they are not interested use another question to find out the real objection.

Cold calling members of the public

Your job may involve cold calling members of the public.

Do not forget to use your customer's name. Invite them to address you by your first name. They may reciprocate.

Tell them that their friend has just bought your product and was delighted with the benefits. They felt that they would be equally delighted. You will probably get a noncommittal response like, "I'm not sure I want to purchase one just yet." Arouse their curiosity by telling them about their friend's experience.

Ask to call around when convenient. Say that you can show them what their friend has bought without any commitment from them. Give them two alternative dates. They will be less likely to refuse. Just say something like, "I could call round on Wednesday or Thursday evening. Which evening would suit you best?"

Perhaps the prospect will be reluctant to meet in their home. If so just arrange to meet in a cafe or hotel or meet them at your own premises. Ask them to get a pen and write down the details. Some people forget the date or time or address after they hang up.

Getting past the secretary

Sometimes it is difficult to get past the receptionist, secretary or personal assistant. Try to build rapport with these people. Use their name. Be polite. It is not what you say that is important. It is how you say it. Do not treat them as an obstacle.

Use the first name of their boss. The secretary will assume that you already know each other. If they do not put you through ask when it will be convenient to call back. State the reason for your call. Ask them to book you the call. Use the opportunity to find out more about the prospect if possible.

An example approach would be:

"Good morning Jane, my name is David Smyth from Uniclear. We have been working with Bolton Glazing for the last six months and have managed to improve their operating efficiencies substantially. Their Managing Director Tim Bradley said we should talk to Peter. When would be a good time to talk to him?"

This way you have quickly introduced yourself and your company. You have established your credentials. You have given the name of a referral of equal rank. The secretary now has the dilemma that she dares not turn away someone who will save the company money. She will probably put you through right away. If not she will at least check with her boss to find out if he will take the call.

Never accept that someone will ring you back.

Keep control over the situation. Never leave the next step under someone else's control. Ask instead for a good time to call back.

If all else fails ring early in the morning or late in the evening. It is unlikely that the secretary will be there. Chances are that your prospect will pick up the phone.

Voice mail

Never leave a message on voice mail if you are cold calling. Try pressing zero to get back to the switchboard. Then ask them to page the person you need.

If someone does not know you they are unlikely to call back.

Only ever leave messages on voice mail if you have an established relationship with an existing customer.

Subsequent contacts

Often it takes several visits before you manage to get the sale. Most sales with new accounts take 5 or more visits before an initial order is placed.

With this in mind you must be patient. Do not give up after the first or second visit. About half of all salespeople do not follow up with a prospect. The business inevitably goes to their more persistent competitors.

Chapter 11. Qualifying the prospect

Qualifying

The first person you contact in a new company may not have the authority to buy your products. Qualify early on their exact level of purchase authority. Make sure that all the decision makers are present when you make your sales presentation.

Be tactful in how you find out their exact purchasing authority.

You do not want the client to feel inferior in any way. You could find out their authority level by asking:

- Who else is involved in the decision making process?
- What is your company procedure for setting up a new supplier?
- How can we go about approving the decision to proceed?
- Are you able to place the order today?

The first person you contact may not be the ultimate decision maker. Make sure that all the decision makers are present when you make your sales presentation.

Never rely on anyone else taking your proposal to the ultimate decision maker.

- Someone else will not have your understanding of your products or services.
- Someone else will not have your passion for the service that you provide.
- Someone else will not have your capacity to overcome objections.

Identify the influencers

Identify the people within your customer's organization who are willing to change. These are the risk takers.

Risk takers are easier to convince.

Risk takers are easier to convince that your products will improve their processes. These people are adept at persuading others. They are the influencers.

Risk takers embrace change. They often have the ear of the senior decision maker. Their enthusiasm often carries the day. They want to perform well. They want to be seen to be making the right decisions and recommendations.

Technical decision makers

Get to know the technical decision makers in your customer's organization.

Technical decision makers decide which products meet company standards.

They are interested in reliability, technical capability and durability. The technical decision maker will draw up a shortlist of acceptable suppliers and products. You need to be on this shortlist.

If you are rejected by a technical decision maker find out the reason. It may be that your product needs some extra specification. Feed this information back to the right people in your own organization.

Technical decision makers cannot say 'yes', but they can and do say 'no'.

Buyers

Buyers are concerned with cost and the price that they must pay.

Buyers don't usually make the initial purchase decision.

Their job is to negotiate the best possible deal for their company.

Finance decision maker

This is the person who controls the purse strings. They will be responsible for setting budgets. They sign off on all major purchases.

The finance decision maker has influence with the most senior person in the organization.

Finance decision makers are analytical. They are interested in the detail of the figures, so that they can corroborate your claims. They are interested in payback, savings or return on investment. They do not make snap judgements or decisions.

Sell them the specifics and the detail.

Joint decision maker

Joint decision makers can recommend your product. They may lead you to believe that they are the final decision maker. As you go for a trial close you may be told that they need to refer the decision to someone else.

In you are in retail sales or selling household products the joint decision maker may be the spouse of the buyer.

Middle management

Middle managers are interested in operational savings. They like proposals that are easy to implement, with minimum disruption to operations. They will show interest if your proposal can make their busy lives simpler.

Ultimate business decision maker

This is the person who decides to buy your products or services. This person is usually the senior manager of the relevant department.

Make sure that you meet this person. Present your products to him. Build rapport with this person. He often has the final decision on which products to use.

Provide a summary of the proposal.

> ***Their decision will be based on logic, not emotion.***

They do not want you to waste their time. They have other more important concerns. Just sell them the hard benefits.

End users

End users are not decision makers. However they are often asked for their opinion. They will be asked about the performance of your products.

This is likely to happen if you already sell some products to the customer.

End users appreciate operational improvement.

Talk to end users in as many working environments as possible. Understand how people use your products. This will help you to develop more ideas on how to sell them.

Get as much product feedback as possible. Draw up a list of questions and record their answers. Find out

- What they like and dislike about the product.
- What they would change to improve the product.
- If they are happy with the maintenance contract.
- If they are happy with the after sales service.
- If they would recommend the product to others.
- If they would buy again if it was up to them.

Pass this information on to your product development or design people. Use the information to help sell the product to others.

Strive to enhance your end user and product reliability knowledge.

Chapter 12. Identifying needs and wants

First impressions

When you meet someone new they will form an opinion on you before you even open your mouth. They will base their opinion on your appearance.

You do not get a second chance to make a first impression.

First opinions are difficult to overcome. You only have a few minutes to do so. Therefore your appearance needs to be right. Dress appropriately for your sales sector. You must look and act the part. Your hair needs to be neatly trimmed. Your shoes need to be polished. Your clothes need to be clean and pressed.

Most important of all you need to be wearing a smile.

A good idea is to dress for the job you want, not the one you have. Think, act and talk like you are one level higher in your organization. Other people in your organization will begin to view you in the same manner.

Your entire product aids such as samples, brochures, presentation files and stationery need to be high quality and in new condition. Replace anything that has become worn.

Set the scene

Begin by telling the customer that you are there to help. Explain that you want to find out about their specific needs. You can then propose a solution that suits their needs. Explain that you want to build a long-term relationship.

An opportunity to impress

Early meetings with potential clients are an opportunity to impress. Be professional and reliable. Provide as good a level of service as possible.

Answer all queries quickly and thoroughly.

Ask for the decision makers to be present

Ask for the decision makers to be present. This is essential if you are going to give a sales presentation. You can then influence the right people directly.

Identify your prospect's needs and wants

People buy products that they need or want. Often they want the product because a friend has endorsed it.

> *If people want something bad enough they will find a way to afford it.*

They will justify the purchase to themselves.

This is why you need to identify the prospect's needs and wants. Ask the right questions. Listen carefully to the answers you receive. Then identify those features that provide the desired benefits.

Understand the customer's motive in buying:

- What benefits are they looking to gain from the purchase?
- What are they afraid of losing?
- What are their major concerns?
- Do they already buy a similar product from someone else?

- Do they want a cheaper product?
- Do they want a better product?
- Do they want a better service level?
- Do they need quicker deliveries?

Asking about problems

***Never offer solutions until you have first found out the problems.**2

Never make assumptions. Never offer a solution until the buyer is first aware that a problem exists. The buyer must first realise the financial implications of the problem. Only then does a proposed solution become an attractive proposition.

Ask the customer about any problems that they are experiencing. You will then know if your products can help the customer. Ask how satisfied they are with their current suppliers. This will unearth any problems. The answer will reveal what is important to the customer in terms of service.

Find out how the problem affects their organization. Estimate how much the problem is costing them. This will show how much your product can save them.

Always ask about the effects when a customer mentions a problem.

Why you should ask questions

Asking questions helps you to connect with people. It helps you to build rapport. You can agree and relate to the answers you get. Just keep your input brief. Let the customer do the talking. Your job is to gather information and to build rapport.

Ask questions to:

- Establish needs and wants.
- Make the customer aware of their needs and wants.

- Make the customer evaluate new information.
- Lead the customer in the desired direction.
- Make the customer understand where they need to improve things.
- Differentiate yourself from your competitors.
- Allow the customer to talk about their interests.
- Move the customer towards closure.
- Evoke their fears.
- Talk about what is important to the customer.
- Talk about the customer's objectives.
- Uncover how the customer would use your products or service.
- Close the sale.

Ask specific questions

Ask specific questions when you meet with existing or prospective customers. Quickly find out their needs. Do this by asking the right questions. Ask questions that will make the customer think. Your questions should be concise and unambiguous. Try to uncover problems that your product can resolve.

Ask about problems, issues, challenges, shortcomings or difficulties they may be facing.

Ask questions such as:

- What level of service do you expect from a supplier?
- What are the most important benefits of the products you use?
- What extra features are important to you?
- What similar products are you buying from competitors?
- What will it take for you to place an order with us?

Needs awareness and the consequences of not buying

First make the customer aware of their needs. You can then sell the benefits of your solution. Some customers are not aware of their needs. Ask the right questions about their problems. This will ensure that they appreciate their needs.

Ask about the implications of the problems that they are facing. Show the consequences for them of not buying your product. They should understand the cost of doing nothing. Show them what the pain will be like. They need to feel that pain. They need to appreciate the financial implications of their current problem.

A small current problem for the client can become a larger problem in the future.

You can add a sense of urgency by pointing out that problems will get worse. If you make the customer aware of their needs you can motivate them to take action *before* you present your proposal.

The prospect of the pain of losing something is much more powerful than the pleasure of gaining something. Be careful how you tackle this issue. Make it clear that your motive is to help the customer overcome any undesired consequences.

People are more responsive if you take the time to identify their needs.

Do not make assumptions

People are unique. They have different perspectives. They see the world in different ways. They do not buy for the same reasons as others.

Find out what these buying motives are. You cannot skip this stage of the process.

Never make assumptions about a prospect's motives if you wish to secure a sale.

Use open questions

Fit your questions into the conversation.

Do not turn the process into an interrogation.

Vary the types of questions you ask. This will avoid the impression of an interrogation.

Use open questions at the beginning to gather information. You do not want simple *yes* or *no* answers. Follow up the open questions with probing questions designed to gather more information.

Open questions all begin with who, what, where, when, which, why and how. Begin every question with one of these interrogative words.

Avoid questions beginning with the word 'why'. Many people find this type of question threatening. They feel that they are forced to defend or justify their view point.

Asking why is usually not conducive to building rapport.

Avoid closed questions

Closed questions begin with words such as 'could', 'should', 'would', 'may', 'can', 'will', 'are' and 'is'. These questions will elicit a straight *yes* or *no* response.

The danger is that the answer can just as easily be 'No'.

You do not want rejection. You do not want to give the customer the opportunity to say 'no.' Drop closed questions from your diction.

Only ever use closed questions to confirm your understanding of what the customer has already told you. Only use a closed question when you already know the answer.

Take notes

Take notes of the answers you get. Jot down the phrases the customer uses. Reflect these phrases back when talking to the customer. Use them later in your sales presentation. Using the same language as the customer helps to build rapport. The customer will feel that you understand their concerns and viewpoint.

Listen

The more customer needs you can uncover the better. Listen actively to what your customer says. Beware of any prejudice that you may harbour. This can filter out or distort the message.

Clients are not always aware of their needs. You may have to dig to get to the information you need.

Strive to appreciate your client's point of view. The more you listen, the more you will learn about your customer.

Repeat and reflect their views in order to build rapport. If you actively listen to your customers they will be more inclined to listen to you.

Establish their resources

Establish the customer's resources before you make your presentation.

- What is their total spend budget?
- How much can they afford to spend on your products?
- How much are they considering spending at this stage?

When you know the answers to these questions you can select the best options for the customer. There is no point trying to sell them something they cannot afford. Select a more suitable alternative. Think about finance options if budgets are limited.

Think about the commitments you may need from the customer. Perhaps they need to make staff available for training on new equipment. Find out about delivery and commissioning constraints. Then make a proposal to match their availability. Incorporate all constraints into your presentation.

What you should find out about the customer

Customers need solutions to their problems. Find out what their problems are. Then show how your products can help solve their problems. Find out:

- What the customer thinks he needs.
- What the customer actually needs.
- What the customer thinks about your products and your company.
- What the customer expects to get from the product or service.
- What the customer feels or thinks is important.
- What the customer thinks about you.
- What the customer thinks about competing products and organizations.
- What the customer values in their current supplier relationships.
- What budget has the customer got?
- When can additional funding be authorised?
- How does the funding needs to be justified?
- How much does the customer expect to pay?
- What credit rating should the customer get?
- Does the customer have the final buying decision?
- Who else is involved in the buying decision?
- Who might block the buying decision?
- Which factors influence the buying decision?

- Which obstacles might block the sale?
- How urgently does the customer need a solution?
- The opportunity cost of not buying the product or service.
- What objections does the customer have?
- How does the customer choose his suppliers?
- Which other suppliers is the customer considering using?
- Any time-line constraints.

Keep a written stock list of questions to unearth information.

Emotions and logic

A customer's emotions dictate if they will buy the product.

Their logic will justify the purchase later. However emotion creates the underlying desire.

Create an emotional attachment between the customer and your product.

Let the customer *feel* what owning the product will be like.

Ask questions that reveal the customer's emotions. Ask about feelings and preferences. Discover and evoke their fear of pain, loss or failure. Appeal to their vanity and ego.

You can use a three-question system based on emotion, logic and emotion to close out a sale. An example would be:

- Can you see how this product would reduce accidents? (Yes- emotional reduction of fear).
- Do you want to reduce accidents? (Yes - logical).
- When would be the best time to begin reducing accidents? (Now – reduces emotional fear).

Create Empathy

Your priority is to create empathy between yourself and the customer.

Customers are unique and need a personalised approach and service.

People are unique. People have different priorities and perspectives. They react differently to circumstances. People have their own views, feelings, values, desires and aims.

You need to understand this if you want to succeed in sales. No two customers are the same.

The only way to attract and keep new customers is to find out and then give them exactly what they want.

If you get to know your customer you will be able to build rapport and trust. This is essential if you are to get the business.

People like to talk about themselves and their viewpoints.

Encourage people to talk about themselves.

Get to know the customer's feelings and concerns. Appreciate the customer's perspective without judgement. Demonstrate that you are sensitive to their feelings. Tune into their wavelength and create resonance. Echo their ideas and feelings. Use similar terms and phrases as your clients. Connect with their thoughts and emotions. Try to reach accord and agreement.

Empathy occurs when:

- You respect the views of the client.
- You respect the needs and concerns of the client.
- You actively listen.
- You show that you are interested in the speaker.

- You show that you value their feelings and attitudes.
- You reassure the client that you care about them and their concerns.
- You are open and responsive in your body language and communication.
- You encourage others to express their feelings.
- You refrain from judgement and apportioning blame.
- You avoid offering unwanted advice.
- You help the client to find a solution that is helpful to them.

By displaying empathy you can build trust. You can get the client to respond positively. The more you care about your customers the stronger the relationships you will build.

You cannot create empathy if the customer feels that you do not care about them.

Building rapport

Displaying empathy with others is the best way to build rapport. Showing a genuine interest in others helps to build rapport. You can build rapport by listening actively to clients, talking about their interests and asking about their progress.

Build rapport with all existing and potential customers.

Try to get on the same wavelength as your clients. Find out and discuss common interests, hobbies, values, beliefs and concerns. Echo back the customer's feelings. Show empathy for their concerns and problems.

Building rapport leads to agreement and cooperation.

Building empathy enables you to strike a deal.

Always begin a conversation with existing customers by asking how they are. Ask about the latest status since you have last met them.

***Building rapport helps to build trust.**†*

With new customers, write down all of their concerns at early meetings. You will need all of this information for your sales pitch. Show that you understand the customer's needs. Empathise with their concerns. Agree the benefits to be delivered. Look at areas where you can remove risk from the customer's mind.

Show them that you care. Show that you want to support them and help satisfy their needs. Sincerely compliment the customer at some stage.

Match and mirror

Match and mirror your customer's body language. Do this by adapting similar posture, gestures and energy levels as the customer. Agree with their beliefs and values.

Talk about their favourite subject

Talk about the customer's favourite subject. This will usually be themselves, their family or their hobby. Perhaps there is a particular sport they like.

***Look for something in common that can help develop a bond.**†*

You will probably see pictures, trophies or certificates displayed in their office. This will give you a starting point.

Ask about those things that they take pride in. Ask them what they would do if they got away from the rat race. Indulge them in their dreams and visions.

People buy products from people they like. This holds even if the products are more expensive.

The next stage

First find out the customer's needs and wants. Next agree the cost of the problem to them. Then move the customer to the next stage of the sales cycle. Your objective may be to:

- Arrange a meeting at which you will give your presentation.
- Arrange a meeting with end users and come back with a proposal.
- Submit a written proposal.

Turn them over to another salesperson

Sometimes, no matter what you do to build empathy, you will find that you cannot progress further with a particular prospect. Perhaps they are not warming to you personally. Rather than lose the sale, turn them over to another salesperson.

This tactic is often used in face-to-face retail sales such as with car salespeople. If the customer is much older or younger than you, turn them over to someone of a similar age group. The customer may feel more relaxed in dealing with someone of their own age.

The tie-down

The tie-down question is used to test the water. The aim is to get later commitment if you can meet their requirements. Ask this question before you arrange to make a sales presentation to the customer.

> ***The tie-down seeks agreement to buy if you can meet the customer's needs.***

An example of the tie-down would be, "If I can show that our proposal will meet all of your needs and the deal is right for you, can we have the business?"

If the answer is yes then you can prepare and give a presentation. If the answer is no, then probe to uncover the objection.

Chapter 13. Written proposals

Sometimes you will be asked to submit a written proposal. Companies whose written proposals are short-listed will be asked to give a presentation.

Focus your written proposal on the customer's needs.

Always ask to give a presentation of the proposal. This gives you the chance to overcome any objections. If your request is turned down ask to ring up after they have read the proposal. This will give you a chance to answer any objections before any decisions are made.

Preparation with the customer

Find out the customer's preferred format for written proposals. Find out:

- Who will be reading the proposal?
- The level of detail required.
- Anything that the customer would like included.
- What the customer does not like to see in a written proposal.

Ask for a copy of a previous winning proposal. This will help you tailor your proposal to the preferred format.

Focus on the customer needs

Focus your written proposal on the customer's needs. Take into account any concerns that they have.

Use the customer's terminology. Repeat any words that the customer used repeatedly in your earlier meetings. Include their company name throughout the proposal.

Substantiate any claims you make. Allow the customer a limited choice of options.

Summarise the benefits of your proposal. Explain why the customer should buy your products. Outline the risk of doing nothing.

Format

Use a standard format for all of your proposals. Include the following:

- Executive summary of the proposal.
- Introduction, outlining the scope and objectives.
- The main issues and problems facing the customer.
- The alternatives that you have considered.
- The pros and cons of each.
- Your findings and recommendations.
- The benefits to the customer.
- The proposal details, including time-line.
- The company investment and resources required.
- The return on investment or payback period.

Layout

The proposal should be easy to read and interpret. Subdivide the proposal into the above sections. Use clear, simple and concise language. Keep sentences and paragraphs short. Use graphics and space to break up the text.

Executive summary

__Write the executive summary last, even though it is included at the start of the proposal.__

Many people only read the executive summary. Therefore make sure that it is well written and self-contained. Include your unique selling point. Include all the benefits of your proposal.

The executive summary should be persuasive.

Submit early

Find out the deadline for submitting the written proposal.

Make sure that your proposal arrives a day or two before the deadline.

If your proposal is the first to arrive, it will probably get more attention. They will spend more time reading it.

Chapter 14. Presenting the product

Your presentation must demonstrate how your product matches the customer's needs or wants.

__The time to win a pitch is before you give it.__

The way to do this is to research, plan, prepare and rehearse.

Know your objective in advance

It is vital to plan your presentation in advance. Research your customer. The larger the customer's organization, the more research you should carry out.

__Identify your desired outcome, which may not always be to get an order.__

Some initial presentations are made to junior buyers before you get an opportunity to pitch to the real decision makers.

Keep the end objective and the associated rewards in mind. This will help to motivate you while preparing and giving the presentation.

Usually the aim is to close the sale there and then. No matter how brilliant your presentation, it will not have been successful unless you close the sale.

Research in advance

Have an agenda. Know which questions to ask. Identify and invite the decision makers.

Research your audience. Ring them up and speak to them in advance. Better still arrange to meet them.

Sit down in advance and cover the issues that are important to each decision maker. Discuss your presentation and what you should include. This will help you to establish rapport. You will also get ownership from them. After all, they have been involved in shaping the presentation. Involving the decision makers beforehand increases the chances of them accepting your proposal.

Understand the customer's attitude towards you and your company. Any past negative experiences with your company will make your task more difficult. Point out any improved procedures and recent product improvements.

Carry out enough research to know more about the subject than anyone in your audience. This will build your credibility. You will be the acknowledged expert on the subject.

Plan in advance

Consider the customer's needs. Plan how you will present the benefits of your offering. Anticipate the likely questions and objections. Work out how to answer these.

You may be asked technical or financial questions which you cannot answer. Do not guess or bluff. This could lose you the sale. Simply jot down the question. Then promise to get back with an answer as soon as possible.

If you have an assistant with you, get them to step out and call the expert in your firm. If not, try to get an answer from your company during any break. Then give the answer at the end of the presentation. This will impress the audience with your professionalism in quickly answering the query.

Understand the customer's motivation for buying.

Only 20% of the sales cycle should be spent presenting your product and trying to close the sale. 80% of your time will be spent establishing needs and wants, building rapport and overcoming objections. Success comes to those who do the proper research and groundwork.

The more research you do, the easier your presentation and closure will be.

Winning a pitch is the end result of a process. It is not a single isolated event.

Bring supporting material

Bring all necessary supporting material including handouts, brochures, testimonials and business surveys.

Bring additional copies. People often turn up at the last minute to sit in on the presentation.

Give out handouts at the end of your presentation. Do not give them out at the start. People will read them instead of paying attention to your presentation. Handouts should contain brief bullet points. Include the main advantages of your product in terms of the customer's needs.

Set up in advance

Set up the room and the equipment in advance. Get there an hour early.

Make sure the facilities are satisfactory. Check that everything is in working order. If something is not working it could take 30 minutes to repair or replace. This leaves enough time to run through your slides and think about what you are going to say.

Make sure that you know how to operate all the equipment. Have technical help on standby in case of equipment failure. Know where you are going to stand. Make sure that you will not be blocking the screen.

Practise in advance

The more you practise at something the better you get. The better you get the more effortless it appears to your audience. The more effortless it appears the more you will be perceived as an expert in your area. Practice builds confidence. It reduces anxiety on the day of the presentation. Practice ensures a winning performance.

Practise giving the presentation to a colleague or your boss. Ask for constructive feedback.

Check how long it takes to give the whole presentation. Summarise the presentation if required. The presentation needs to be shorter than the allotted time slot.

You must allow time to answer questions, overcome objections and close the sale.

Presenting as a team

If you are presenting to a group bring your own experts. They can answer questions on technical areas. They can explain how issues such as financing and distribution will be handled.

If you are presenting as a team make sure that you practise together.

You need to be a cohesive force, not a group of individuals. Everyone must be consistent in their approach. If individual members prepare their own section, review this as a group. Make changes as needed to ensure consistency of approach.

Each presenter needs to add value. Clearly define who is responsible for each section. Do not cover common ground. Rehearse the hand overs. They need to be smooth. Agree who will handle any questions and objections.

There should be no ad-libbing on the day of the presentation.

Each member should stick to the script. During the presentation, team members should support one another. Do this by using suitable body language. When answering questions refer to supporting information provided other speakers.

Confidence

Confidence is crucial when giving a presentation. You must believe in yourself, your products and in what you are saying. If you have any doubts then why should the customer buy?

If you have researched, planned and practised in advance, why shouldn't you succeed?

It is important to realise that the client wants your presentation to be good. They are on your side. They are hoping that your offering will answer their problems. If it does not, then they will be no further forward. They will have to invest time and energy with someone else.

The customer has already invested a great deal in you. They are hoping to get a return on their investment. Therefore do not be anxious about giving the presentation. Providing that you have prepared and rehearsed properly everything will go well.

Passion

Passionate salespeople win business. Their enthusiasm influences customer decisions. They sincerely believe that they are offering the ideal solution. If you don't fully believe in your offering, the customer will not be convinced that they should buy.

Enthusiasm

If you do not sound enthusiastic you will have little chance of securing a sale. Use your voice to convey your enthusiasm for your products, your service and your job.

Alter the tone and pitch of your voice to inject enthusiasm.

Enthusiasm is infectious. It spreads to those around you. How do you become enthusiastic? Try smiling more.

Structure and layout of your presentation

- Your presentation should be well structured, clear and precise.
- It should be easy to follow.
- It should focus on the customer.
- It should concentrate on your unique benefits.
- It should be delivered professionally.
- It should include as much customer participation as possible.

Your presentation should follow a set pattern.

- Begin with a brief introduction of yourself, your team, your company and your offering.
- Tell your audience how long the presentation will take.
- Explain how you will deal with questions.
- Explain the objectives of the presentation.
- Outline briefly what you will be covering.
- The main section should concentrate on your unique selling point.
- Include a practical demonstration if possible.
- Invite questions and overcome any objections

- Finish by recapping the two or three main benefits of your proposal.
- Ask for commitment to the sale or the next stage of the process.

Presentation technique

Follow these guidelines to improve your presentation technique:

- Stand up when giving your presentation.
- Keep your head erect and your shoulders back.
- Direct your energy at the audience.
- Include all of the audience.
- Address each member by name.
- Do not talk to the screen.
- Engage your audience and hold their interest.
- Establish and maintain eye contact.
- Remember to smile.
- Do not shuffle about, you will appear anxious.
- Do not fidget with pens, pointers or other objects.
- Speak up when talking to a group.
- Talk in a conversational tone.
- Use open body language.
- Use hand gestures to help emphasise your points.

Your voice projects better when standing up. You come across as being more dynamic. You will also have more vitality. You will be able to deal with questions better.

Make eye contact with each member of the audience in turn. Do not concentrate on one individual. The decision making process is usually shared.

Visual aids

Be aware of the limitations and disadvantages of visual aids:

- Do not use too many slides or screens.
- Keep backgrounds consistent.
- Use a uniform format and typeface.
- Keep the information on the screen summarised.
- Use no more than 30 words on any slide.
- Concentrate on the main selling points.
- Stick to one main selling point per slide.
- Do not clutter the screen with tables of figures.
- Allow time to look at each screen before you move on to the next one.
- Do not let the information become a substitute for your presence.
- Do not simply read from the screen.
- Use different phrases from the words on the screen.
- Add extra supporting information to what is included on the screen.

Your visual aids should not simply be a prompt for what you are going to say.

Do not display a screen until you are ready to talk about it.

People will read ahead. When they do so they will not be listening to what you say. This will hamper your capacity to influence them.

Use visual aids to illustrate a point. They are ideal way of showing the workings of a product.

When closing, switch off the visual aids and sell the merits of your proposal. This reduces distractions.

Presenting to a group

If you are presenting to a group sell to them all. Include a summary for the CEO, facts and figures for the finance person and graphics for the technical person.

You need to get them all on board.

One dissenting voice and you could lose the sale. Get yourself introduced to everyone before the presentation. Concentrate on anyone that you have not met before. Make sure you get their business cards, or otherwise remember their names. Use their names as you involve them during the presentation.

Concentrate on the leader while giving the presentation.

If you get the leader on board the others usually follow.

If you already have rapport with the buyer, get him to speak up in your favour early on.

From the start get interaction from as many people as you can. It keeps them involved. It produces a feeling of ownership. It prevents them from switching off.

Get to the point quickly

Get to the point quickly. Introduce your unique selling point within the first five minutes. This prevents your audience from switching off.

Dealing with questions

Let the audience know that they can ask questions during the presentation.

Some questions take too long to answer during the presentation. Just write the question on the board as a reminder. Then answer it at the end.

You may get a question that you plan to answer later in your presentation. Just tell the person that you will be covering that topic later.

Dealing with objections

If someone seems unenthusiastic, draw out their objections early on. Write each of their objections down. Deal with them in turn. This will sway people in your direction.

Ask for any other objections or anticipated problems from your audience. Write these down and deal with them all.

Engage in dialogue

The presentation should not be a monologue. Involve your audience in your presentation. Use their names. Ask them questions. Make them think. Keep them involved.

Physically involve them

Have your audience do something. Let them try out the product or at least hold the samples.

> ***If they touch and feel the product they become emotionally involved. They develop a feeling of ownership.***

The more audience participation you can get the better. Ask them to help with set up. Ask them to help give out handouts. The more you involve people the less they will discuss or think about unrelated issues.

Do not just tell, demonstrate

Demonstrate the benefits of the product in use if possible. Let the client push the buttons and operate the machine. The more the client is involved in the demonstration the better.

Take the client through several simple exercises. Select exercises that demonstrate important features for the client.

Make the process progressively more challenging and you will have them hooked.

Encourage the client. Tell them that they have picked up the skill very quickly. Point out those features which provide the required benefits.

Involve them emotionally.

Get the customers talking about what they like the best. Ask them ownership questions. This makes them think about how it would feel to own the equipment.

Remove the equipment from the client at the end of the demonstration. If they ask to see or use it again, then this is a buying signal.

Become an expert

Knowledge is power. Know all the features and benefits of your products and those of the competition. Being an expert will improve your presentation.

Learn everything there is to know about your products. Be fully versed in any current marketing strategies and advertising programmes.

Learn as much as possible about your own company. Know who to contact to answer technical or financial questions. Know who to contact to solve any problems for your customer.

Know your competitors

You need to know about your industry. Learn everything you can about your competitors. Be familiar with their management and sales structure. Be familiar with their products and their pricing structures.

Get hold of your competitor's products and try them out.

Get your company's marketing department to benchmark competitor products. Get a full report drawn up on all the main competitor products. Compare all the features and benefits. Compare pricing, running costs, maintenance needs, durability, etc.

Study the competitor's sales literature. Find out how they like to pitch their products. Prepare counterarguments.

Talk to customers who have dealt with your competitors. If needs be you can pose as a potential new customer. Ask about their experiences. You may unearth problems with competitor products. Use this information when comparing your products to their offering.

Get to know all of your competitor's weaknesses.

Point out where your own products are superior. Be aware of the advantages and disadvantages of your own products compared with your competitors.

Anticipate all of the possible questions you might be asked. Prepare so that you can answer these questions with confidence.

Know your customer

Every company considers themselves to be unique.

Clients do not want to sit through a standard presentation that you have given to dozens of others.

Take the time to consider the customer's individual needs. Unless you tailor your offering to meet these needs you will not be successful.

Read the company's latest published annual report.

Read the company's mission statement. Check out the areas in which the company is investing. Look at their short and medium term goals.

The report will have a chairman's statement. There will be short autobiographical information on the members of the board. These people will be the key decision makers. You will probably be pitching to the people working for them. They will follow their lead.

Find out all you can about the customer before giving your presentation.

Remember that you are selling to people, not a company. People decide whether or not to buy. People have their own unique hopes, beliefs, needs and wants. Discover what these are. Then demonstrate how you can meet them with your products.

Talk to other suppliers or people who have worked with the company.

There will be other non-competitive suppliers out there. Discreetly get this information from the buyer or the customer services department. Ask these suppliers how they managed to secure the business. Find out what they know about the buyers and their preferences.

Find out about the decision makers.

Meet with the company decision makers. Find out how they like to do business:

- Do they like to have all the detail or is a summary of more interest to them?
- Are they cautious or do they like to take calculated risks?
- Are they more interested in performance or the savings involved?
- Do they want to get one over on their competitors?
- Do they like to be the market leaders in investing in new technology?

Answers to questions like these indicate how to pitch the benefits of your products. Use compelling arguments. Back them up with facts.

Know why they buy

Understand the triggers which cause your customers to place an order. Business decision makers decide to buy once they have been convinced that your product:

- Will make them money.
- Will save them money.
- Will save them time.

They also need convincing that:

- The product or service is reliable.
- You will provide excellent after sales service.

Build this information into your presentation. Concentrate on these points in your summary.

Keep it simple

Keep your presentation short, simple and easy to understand.

Aim to close the sale in fifteen minutes.

If you go much beyond fifteen minutes your audience will switch off. Your customer just wants the facts as they pertain to their interests. Do not overload your audience. They will lose concentration. They will remember little of what you have covered.

It is not what you put into the presentation that counts. It is what the customer takes out of it that is critical.

It is what the customer remembers that counts.

Concentrate on those few key facts that will sway the customer's judgement. Highlight the key benefits of your proposal. This is critical if other companies are presenting. The decision will not be made until later. The customer will need to remember these key facts later. Help them to remember by repeating, reinforcing and summarising the key points at the end.

Stick to your time limit. Concentrate on the customer's needs and wants. Begin by talking about the customer's problems and needs. Explain why your offering is important to them. Explain how your product or service can satisfy their needs. You may include a short demonstration at this stage. Do not cover every feature and do not use complicated technical terminology. Stick to those specific benefits that meet the customer's needs.

Authenticate your claims

Include endorsements from satisfied customers.

One testimonial is better than one hundred promises.

Tell a story of how you have solved a similar problem for another customer. Customers hate to be guinea pigs. They prefer to know that the solution is tried and tested. The less risk the better.

Stories are easier to remember and they will authenticate your claims.

Include a list of satisfied customers with your handouts. Industry awards or registered memberships of trade associations help to reinforce your company's credentials.
Perhaps you have a copy of a professional or trade magazine article on your company.

Explain the impact that your product will have on their company. Point out your excellent after sales record. Invite questions, which will be objections or reservations of some sort. Answer these. Use a suitable closing technique. Then ask for the sale.

Limit the choices available

Do not offer too big a choice.

If you give a customer too many choices they have difficulty coming to a decision.

If there are too many options the customer will worry about making the wrong choice. They worry that they will regret any choice they make.

Faced with too many choices customers opt for the safest course of action, which is to do nothing.

At the same time you should offer some flexibility. Recommend two choices to the customer based on your interpretation of their needs.

If you only offer a single choice you limit the customer to a take it or leave it option. The danger is that they will leave it. If you offer two choices there is a much better chance the customer will select one.

Offer flexibility

Build flexibility into your proposal. Give the option to review the service as you go along. This reduces the risk in the buyer's mind.

For example you might agree to supply 1000 widgets each month. In this case offer to increase or reduce the volume by 25% according to the customer's demand.

Take one step at a time

The selling process involves incremental commitments from the customer at each stage.

Guide the customer along these stages. At each stage you need to get agreement and a commitment to go to the next stage. You cannot skip stages unless you receive early buying signals.

Features

Never concentrate on selling features. Perhaps you are a salesperson in a music store. When demonstrating a music system it is pointless talking endlessly about features. Most customers are confused by technical features. The second problem is that you do not know which features are of interest to the customer.

> ***People do not buy features, they buy benefits.***

So if you want to demonstrate features first ask which features are of interest to the customer. Then link these features to the benefits that they will bring.

> ***Do not let the customer get hung up on features.***

If you do this the customer will ignore all products which lack the desired features. They will first narrow their search and then decide on price. If you do not have a product with their wish-list of desired features they will leave and go elsewhere.

Sell the benefits

Always concentrate on the benefits and results for the customer. If you do discuss features, then talk about the associated benefits for the customer.

Benefits satisfy customer needs. Lead with your product's capacity to satisfy needs. Establish the customer's needs first. Then sell them the benefits of the product or service. Show them how the product will help them to get the results they want. Concentrate on what the product can do for them.

Do not list more than five benefits at one time. The customer will not be able to absorb any more than that.

> *The first and the last item are easier for the customer to remember.*

Place the benefits that are most important to the customer first and last in the list.

Advantages

Compare your product to what the customer currently uses or what the competitors supply. Ask the customer what they currently use and who supplies it. Then point out the advantages of your product over what they currently use.

If the customer believes that you product offers more benefits for the same price then they will buy from you.

Limitations

Your product may have certain limitations when compared with competitor products. Work out how to get around these limitations. Learn how to minimise these in the customer's mind.

Unique selling point

Convey your unique selling point to the customer.

You will have some unique feature or service that your competitors cannot supply.

Sell the benefit of this to the customer. Ask them if this feature would be important to them.
This reinforces the point and commits them to acknowledging this benefit of your product.

Pay back

Cost your proposal in terms of the pay back for the customer's investment. Express this in terms of the return on investment. This is time it takes to payback the investment with savings gained. After this period the customer profits from the investment.

You may be able to get this information from your existing customers.

Make it easy to pay

Offer easy payment terms and suitable finance packages. Make it easier for the customer to say yes.

Focus on the customer

Focus your sales pitch on the customer. Forget your own needs, wants and problems. Only present information that will be of interest, benefit or concern to the customer.

You can give a brief introductory summary of your company. Limit this to two or three sentences. Focus most of your presentation on issues of direct concern to your customer. They are mainly concerned with what you can do for them.

Customers do not care that your company is the biggest, fastest expanding, most profitable, or longest established. They do not care about all the bells and whistles of your products.

Customers just want to know:

- Does your product meet their needs and wants?
- Is the price competitive?
- Can you deliver on time?
- Can you provide good customer service?

Concentrate on answering these issues and you will close the sale.

Dealing with interruptions

You are likely to be interrupted if you give the presentation at the customer's premises. There could be a phone call for a member of the audience. Perhaps a secretary will ask for a participant to step out for a minute.

Deal with all interruptions calmly. Remain professional. Do not show any irritation. You should know your material well enough. Interruptions should not put you off your stride.

> ***Re-establish the emotional attachment you had before the interruption.***

The interruption will spoil the moment. You will lose the emotional attachment that you have been building. When you resume your presentation you will have to recap on those benefits.

Offer full back up

Offer the full back up of your company. Offer after sales service, technical advice and customer care. Include testimonial letters that authenticate this point.

The importance of price

Price does nothing to add to your credibility.

Price has a limited impact on securing the sale.

Price is not the most important factor when customers make the buying decision. Less than 15% of consumers will buy the cheapest product every time. Less than 1% of consumers will always buy the most expensive product. Everyone else is looking for the best value for money.

Do not move on price to secure new business.

Dropping the price devalues your product in the customer's mind. You will come across as desperate to get the business. Have confidence in your company's pricing structure. Never apologise for the price of your products. Concentrate instead on demonstrating value for money.

Find out the customer's budget in advance. Find out how much they are willing to pay. Offer a product that is in the right price range. Alternatively look at methods of providing finance to spread the payments.

Reduce the risk involved

If your product involves a large investment then lessen the risk involved. Offer a trial period. This allows the customer to experience the benefits for themselves. If you were offering a consultancy service you could offer to provide the service for a limited time and budget. Just get an undertaking to review the relationship after six months.

Buying signals

You may start to get buying signals before you have finished your sales presentation. Go for the trial close. If this works close the sale and abandon the presentation. Job done.

Do not continue with the presentation. You may lose the sale by doing this. There is a danger that you will say something that makes the customer reconsider.

Sensory language

People remember and communicate using different senses. Some people are visually influenced. Others are mainly auditory influenced. Still others like to touch and feel the product.

If someone uses phrases such as, "I see what you mean," or "That looks good enough to me," then they are visually influenced.

Auditory influenced people will say something like, "I hear what you are saying," or "That sounds familiar enough."

People who are influenced by feeling will say something like, "I just cannot get a handle on it," or "We need to get a grip on these costs."

When dealing with people, establish their dominant sensory language. Use the same format when communicating with them.

Incorporate all three sensory formats in your presentation and the language that you use.

If you are presenting to a group use all three sensory formats. For example ask if they can see the benefits. Then later ask if they can feel a difference when demonstrating the product. Ask if an argument sounds right to them.

Start and finish well

It is important that you start and finish well. The audience will remember these parts most. This is due to the primacy and recency effect.

Many people like to have the information placed in context before discussing the detail. They like to see the global picture first. So at the start include an overall picture of the problem.

At the end summarise 4 or 5 main points that you want them to remember.

Leave a working model

At times you will be competing with presentations from other companies. In this case make a working model of your product. After the presentation leave it with the buyer. Give the model to the most senior member of the decision making panel. This will create emotional attachment to your product. It will impress the buyer with your professionalism.

Review each presentation

Take time to review each presentation that you give. Do this with other members of your team as soon as possible after the presentation.

Think about the improvements you can make for your next presentation.

Make a note of what went well and what did not go well. Where there any questions that surprised you? Where you unprepared for some objections? Did you include detail that did not interest the customer? Did you omit something that was of importance to the customer? Do your products lack some critical benefit for the customer?

Incorporate any suggested improvements into future presentations.

Chapter 15. Dealing with objections

Welcome objections

Objections are good.

Objections are a sign that the customer is interested.

Objections show the customer is considering buying your product. They just need reassurance that they are making the right choice.

Objections help you to understand the client's needs better. You need to answer all the customer's objections to their satisfaction. This will remove the objections. It will remove any doubts that might have lingered. You can then lead the customer to the sale.

Reasons for objections

There are various reasons why someone may raise an objection:

- They have misunderstood something you said.
- They need more information to help them make a decision.
- They need more time to decide whether or not to buy.
- They need just one final reason to convince them to buy.
- They do not have the authority to buy.
- They cannot afford it without financial help.
- They are stalling so that they can see a competitor's offering first.
- They want a better price or deal.
- They know your product is inferior to a competitor's in some aspect.
- They fear the risk involved.
- They are not convinced of the benefits.
- They lack confidence in you, the product, or your company.
- They would prefer to spend their money on something else.

- The do not like to betray their loyalty to their existing supplier.
- They have a genuine concern.
- They just do not want to buy.

You need to find out what the exact objection is before you can answer it. Ninety percent of the time the customer will not volunteer the real reason straight away. They will give a stalling statement. This is designed to turn you away without tackling the real issue. People do this to avoid open confrontation.

People are reluctant to point out inferiorities in your product. They do not want face-to-face confrontation. They would rather say something like, "Let me think about it."

Stalling objections

A stalling objection is one in which the objector is hiding the real problem.
There are many common stalling objections. None of the following give you the real reason for not wanting to buy:

- Let me think about it.
- I need to talk to my partner.
- We need to get three quotes first.
- Come back next quarter.
- The budget is spent.
- I'm happy with my current supplier.
- No, thanks, not today.
- Can you send a brochure?
- It is too expensive.

You may get a non-committal objection. If so dig deeper to get to the real problem. You need to understand the underlying cause of the objection. You can then answer the objection to the customer's satisfaction.

Why you get objections

Sometimes the objection occurs because you have not carried out a previous stage of the sales cycle correctly. Worse still, you may have skipped a stage. The problem may be that:

- You have not qualified the buyer correctly.
- You have not uncovered the real needs.
- You have not explained all the benefits.
- You have failed to build enough rapport.
- You, the product or your company lack credibility.
- You have not built trust.
- You used too much logic and not enough emotional appeal.
- You did not stress the negative cost of not buying.
- You missed something in your presentation.

If you do not do your job correctly you will invite multiple objections.

Record objections

Make a note of every objection you receive. Ask you sales team about objections from customers in other areas.

Think of and write down two possible answers to every conceivable objection.

Include these in a workbook. Distribute it to the whole sales team. Work as a group to rehearse your answers to these objections. You can use these answers when dealing with customers.

After your first year in the business you should have heard just about every objection there is. You should also have worked out how to deal with them all.

Overcoming objections is the passport to success.

Anticipate the objections

Anticipate the objections in advance and be ready with your answers. Prepare as thoroughly for the objections as you prepare for the presentation itself.

Have supporting material with you to help answer objections.

Use supporting material such as:

- Cost of ownership comparisons.
- Statistical results of satisfaction surveys.
- Referrals from satisfied customers.
- Independent reviews of your products.

Prevention is better than a cure

Overcome the objections before they occur. Steel their thunder. Include the answers in your presentation.

If you are getting a lot of objections then review your presentation techniques. Perhaps there are some points you need to include up-front.

Include supporting material to authenticate your claims. This dissolves the doubt in the client's mind. It provides the client with the needed reassurance. It provides information the buyer can quote to others who may question the purchase.

Confidence

Display confidence when dealing with objections. This adds to your credibility. Do not appear nervous or hesitant. This will arouse suspicion.

Remain calm, smile and answer with confidence. Say something like, "I'm glad you asked that. I probably need to explain a little more. Can you tell me exactly what your concern is?"

Listen carefully

Give the customer your undivided attention. Uncover the real objection to your proposals. You cannot do this while completing forms, sending texts or thinking about your next question. Listen to the emotional elements of the objection. Try to get a feel for its importance.

Show interest in the speaker and what is being said. Do not interrupt the client. Do not finish his sentences or phrases. Do not jump to conclusions. Let the customer tell their own story. Do not change the subject. Hear them out. Study their body language. Work out their frame of mind.

Clarify the objection

If a customer raises an objection you need to find the root cause. Ask probing questions to get to the real objection.

You must get to the root cause of the objection before you can deal with it.

The customer will not normally present you with the real objection up-front. You will have to dig for it.

The customer might say something like, "I do not know, I'm not sure." This shows that they are interested, but have not yet committed. You should reply with, "I can see that you are very interested. Can you explain exactly what it is that you are not sure about?" This will uncover extra information about the customer's needs and objections.

Get the customer to clarify the reason for the objection. Do this by asking the right questions. Find out why they have voiced a concern. It could be a misunderstanding that you can clear up.

Feed the objection back

Acknowledge the objection by saying something like "Thank you for raising that issue. It is important that I answer it to your satisfaction."

Then restate the objection and get the client to confirm that this is the problem. You need to understand exactly what the issue is before you deal with it.

Dealing with the wrong objection will get you no closer to the sale.

Write down the objection

Always write down the objection. This shows that you are listening.

Writing down the objection shows that you care. It shows that you are taking the objection seriously.

Just say something like, "OK. Just let me make a note of that. It is important that we deal with this to your satisfaction." This buys you time to think about the best way of dealing with the objection.

Isolate the objection

Isolate the objection before dealing with it.

Ask the customer if this is their only concern.

If the objection is the real concern they will answer that it is the only problem. If they are just giving an excuse you may hear the real objection when they answer your question.

If you isolate the objection, you will have moved them closer to the buying decision.

If it is their only objection, then you will get the sale if you can answer it to their satisfaction. You have both agreed in advance that it is the only obstacle remaining to the sale.

You must answer all objections if you are to close the sale.

If there is more than one objection then list them all down.

Get a commitment to the sale

Try at this stage to get a commitment to the sale. Say something like, "If I can answer this objection to your satisfaction, will we then be OK to go ahead?" If the answer is 'no' then find out what the extra objections are.

Empathise with the customer

After listening to, clarifying and isolating the objection there is a further stage required before answering.

Do not go straight to answering the objection.

This may seem like the obvious next step, but it is not.

By raising an objection the customer has taken up an opposing stance.

You must first get the customer back on side. Do this by relating to their concerns. You need to be on the same side as the customer.

The customer is not open to persuasion while they have taken an opposing stance.

You need to align yourself with their position before you can continue.

Find a point of agreement. Agree with their thought process, but not the objection. You must be seen to be working together to solve a common problem. Show that you understand, appreciate and care about their concern. By implication you care about them as a person. By doing this you support their concern.

You could say something like "I understand your concern about service levels. It is very important to us that our customer's needs are met. Some of our most important customers had initial concerns about service. However when they tried our product they found out that......."

With this method you are showing empathy. You are moving away from confrontation by mentioning others with the same issue. You are stating that the majority of customers are satisfied with the service.

You should notice the customer visibly relaxing when you align with their concerns. This will be a sign that you can continue with the sale.

Answer the objection

Having clarified and isolated the objection and re-established empathy you need to supply a satisfactory solution. How you respond depends on the specifics of the objection.

Answer the objection fully to the satisfaction of the client.

It may be that you need to clear up a misunderstanding, sell more features, sell the overall service or give a deal on price.

Agree with the concern, but outweigh the objection with contradicting evidence.

Redirect the objection by saying something like, "That's fine. Now let's see what we can do to make this right for you." This statement opens the customer to the possibility that things can be right.

Then give overwhelming counter benefits to the single objection. This reminds the customer of the total value of the proposal. Point out the emotional benefits. Also point out the pain of not continuing at this stage.

The next chapter outlines how to overcome typical objections.

Techniques to answer objections

There are several standard tools and techniques that will help answer objections, including:

- Prevention by including the answer in your presentation.
- Similar situations where the customer was satisfied.
- Testimonials and references.
- Independent published articles about the quality of your products.
- A cost comparison analysis.
- An independent product review preferably comparing you with the competition.
- Facts and figures to support your claims.
- Details of how you have improved your products, service, facilities or processes.

Confirm that the client is satisfied

Answer the objection. Then check that the customer is happy with your solution. You cannot proceed until the customer has dealt with the objection in his own mind.

If a concern remains there will be no sale.

If the customer is happy with your solution move to close the sale.

If the customer is not satisfied with your answer identify what the remaining problem is. Unless you can fully address the objection you will leave doubt in the buyer's mind.

Go for the test close or assumptive close

Once you have overcome the objections go for the trial close.

If you have answered all the objections you should be able to close out the sale.

Go all out with any referrals, references or testimonials if needs be. Now is the perfect time to close.

The trial close is designed to confirm interest from the client.

Having used the trial close, say nothing until you get a response from the client.

Chapter 16. Typical objections

Typical objections involve the following:

- The price.
- Resistance to change.
- Loyalty to the existing supplier.
- Concerns about features.
- Concerns about after sales support.
- Timing of delivery, installation or commissioning.

"We've spent the budget."

Find out if this is the only objection. If so then you have a good chance of getting the sale. You just need to get the client some finance. Suggest the following:

- Code the sale to a different, but similar budget category.
- Get authority from their boss to overspend on the budget.
- Arrange finance.
- Get the sale now, sign the paperwork, but invoice and deliver later.
- Offer a deferred payment plan.

"It is too expensive."

If the customer believes the product is too expensive they do not feel the gains outweigh the cost involved.

> *You have not matched enough benefits with their needs.*

Price is often the subject of negotiation. Dealing with price should be the last stage of the process. If you get price as the first objection ask to sit it to one side until you have dealt with all other concerns.

Having dealt with all other objections you can return to the only remaining concern which will be the price.

Sell the full benefits of the product before you discuss price.

Selling the full benefits increases the perceived value to the customer. It helps to justify the price before any negotiations.

Begin by asking why the price is too high.

You need to clarify the price objection. The customer may mean that:

- They can get it cheaper elsewhere.
- They do not have enough money.
- It costs more than they expected.
- They want you to give a discount.
- They do not have the authority to spend that much.
- They will look good to their boss by getting a discount.
- The need reassurance before spending so much.
- They do not want the product.

Get the customer to be specific about their objection. Probe deeper to get to the real concern. Find out how much the customer can afford to spend. Then try to close the gap.

Perhaps the price is above their approval level. Suggest that you can issue two or three invoices each of which is within their sign-off authority level. Perhaps you could invoice installation and commissioning separately from the price of the equipment itself.

Ask if they would buy today if the price was right.

Isolate the price as the only problem. Then ask if they would take delivery right away if the price was right.

Ask about their current provider. Then show them added benefits that you can provide. You will know the price from the current provider. Discuss the differential and not the absolute prices. So if your car is £23,000 and the competitor's car is £22,000 you talk about a £1000 difference. You only need to justify the *extra* cost in terms of added quality, features or benefits.

Show how little extra this cost is over the lifetime of the product. So if the customer is paying over a four-year finance deal they are financing an extra £250 each year or £21 each month or just less than £5 each week or 70 pence each day.

If this does not convince them re-establish the value of your offering in terms of benefits, features and quality. Talk about service levels and guarantees that you can provide. Then tackle the issue of price by giving a sweetener. Say something like:

- You can pay over an agreed period.
- We can offer discount for bulk buy.
- I can give you an introductory offer as a new customer.
- We have a sale coming up soon do I can book your orders for that period.

"I'll think about it."

This objection is a stalling tactic. It does not explain the real problem. This objection shows the customer does not value your product or your company. They are not convinced about the benefits. You will only reinforce this belief if you move on price.

Begin by agreeing with the customer. Say something like, "it is important to take the time to make the right decision."

Ask what it is that they need to think about. Find out exactly what their needs are. Then highlight the related benefits of your product. If they are worried about price, deal with this as advised in the previous section.

Ask for the specific issues. Ask for all the problems. Ask if the customer will proceed if you can answer all their concerns. Go through each concern or objection. Answer them in turn. Check each time that you have answered the objection to the customer's satisfaction.

"It is not my responsibility."

If you get this answer you have not qualified the prospect correctly. Just get the details of the right contact. Then ring up using your first contact as a referral.

"I'm too busy."

If they say that they are too busy ask for a convenient time to call back. Do not try to proceed if the client is preoccupied with other concerns. They will not be open to persuasion.

Explain that you have a worthwhile proposal that can save them money or improve their operations. Explain that your call will take less than ten minutes.

"Just send me a brochure."

Some people will try to brush you off by asking you to send a brochure. If you do send one it will end up in the bin.

Just say that you would like to ask a few questions so you can then refer them to the right products in the brochure.

Having got the needed information, offer to take them through the brochure in person. This way you can point out all the benefits that your products can provide for them. If the customer insists on you sending the brochure first, then at least get an agreement to a follow up meeting.

The least you can accept is that you will make a follow up phone call.

"I do not think I really need it."

The customer does not feel an emotional need to own the product. Re-emphasise the benefits and show how they meet the customer's specific needs. Highlight the risks of not buying the product from your company.

The risk associated with not buying is always a stronger motivating cause in the decision to buy.

"I do not think it is good enough for what I need."

There is a perceived problem with the quality. Alternatively the customer feels the product is lacking in some features that he needs.

Probe deeper to discover the real problem. Perhaps you need to offer a different product with more features.

Show the customer written references and testimonials from satisfied customers.

"No. I'm not interested."

Ask the customer to be more specific. What is it that they want? What do they not like about your offering? What would it take to make them interested?

"I'm happy with my current supplier, thank you."

Ask what they like most about their current supplier's offering. This tells you what is important to the customer. It will suggest how you should continue.

Ask what they would change about their current supplier arrangement.

You will gain a foothold if you can offer what they are missing as part of your package. Most customers are not totally satisfied with their suppliers. Unearth the reason for this dissatisfaction. Then offer an alternative superior service.

Often the customer will have been with the current supplier for a long time. It's probably a while since they have looked at the alternatives. They may not realise the advantages of your product offering. You must point these advantages out. Explain that your offering presents value for money with a quality product and service.

Ask to give your presentation.

Suggest that the customer should spread his risk by having more than one supplier.

Perhaps you can get a trial order. Explain that the customer should have a second supplier for price comparison. This will keep his current vendor competitive. Failing that you can promise to supply the customer in emergencies when his current supplier does not have the stock.

Give examples of other customers who take supply from yourself and their current supplier.

Say something like, "So if I can show that we can provide a better overall service at a more competitive offering will you consider doing business with us?"

"Call me in a few months."

This is just a stalling tactic when the client means no. Find out what the real objection is and deal with it.

Ask what will be different in a few months. Ask what is preventing them doing business today.

There may be a genuine problem. Perhaps their stocks are too high. In this case try to get the order now for delivery later.

Perhaps they will have extra funds available in a few months. Again get the order now for later delivery and invoice. Promise current pricing to secure the deal.

Point out the advantages of ordering now. Build in a sense of urgency. Tell the customer that your stocks are good, but supply is limited. Warn them that prices are going up soon. Offer to hold the price. Add in some extras on the condition that they close the deal now.

"What happens if it breaks?"

Point out the product reliability. Give written references and independent product reviews. Point out warranty options, guarantee periods, service facilities, etc.

"I need the opinion of a colleague."

If the customer needs the opinion or authority of a colleague you may not have done your qualifying properly. Just arrange to repeat your demonstration when both are present.

Ask if the customer would buy now if he had total authority to do so. If not, then get his objections. Deal with each of them. This way you have him on board before the second meeting.

Ask the client to recommend the product to his colleagues when you give the second demonstration. Get more detail about the second decision maker. This will help you to prepare before the second demonstration.

"I need to shop around/I need two other quotes"

Prepare in advance a cost comparison with competitor products. Show the customer the written evidence.

First empathise with the customer. Say that it is important to get the best value for money. Point out the time and effort needed to get extra quotes. Ask if he would be happy to proceed if you can show that your product offers the best value for money. If he agrees just produce your cost comparison literature.

Back this up with testimonial material and independent product reviews.

"I need to see the competitor's demonstration."

If the customer wants to see the competition first just agree with the idea. Ask which company will be demonstrating. Point out the unique selling point of the opposition. This shows that you are not worried about the competition.

Ask for a short meeting after the customer has seen all the demonstrations and before he has made a final decision. This will give you a last chance to close the sale.

"I need to talk to my spouse."

You often get this objection in a retail sales environment. The best way to deal with this is to put time pressure on the sale.

Once the customer leaves there is little chance of them returning.

If you want the sale you need to close it there and then.

You could say that this is the last product and you cannot hold it without a deposit. You could say that the price is due to go up tomorrow. This is the last chance to buy at the current price.

You may be demonstrating products in a client's own home. In this case ask in advance if there is a spouse. Then make sure that both partners are available for the demonstration.

What not to do when overcoming objectives

- Never make assumptions. Get the actual reason for the objection.
- Never argue the point.
- Never attack the person. Separate the issue from the person.
- Never avoid the issue. If there is an objection, you must deal with it.
- Do not blame anyone else for the issue. It is your responsibility to resolve it.
- Never tell the customer that they are wrong.
- Do not dwell too long on an objection. Resolve it and move on.
- Never bluff the customer. If you do not know the answer, take a note and tell the customer when you will get back to them. Then ensure that you do.

You can win arguments, but not without damaging the relationship.

Chapter 17. Buying signals

Knowing when customers are ready to buy

If you want to close sales then you need to recognise the buying signals.

You need to know when the customer is ready to buy. You need to spot the signs in their body language or in what they say. The customer will be clearly sending these signals. You need to recognise these signals and close the sale.

Customers will go through three stages in the buying process.

- First they will express an interest.
- Then they will develop a desire.
- Finally they will imagine the benefits of owning the product.

When they get to the third stage, they are ready to buy.

Close the sale immediately when you receive the buying signal.

Close out when you get the chance. Then say as little as possible until you have the sale. If you continue to talk the customer may change his mind because of something you say.

Buying signals

At some stage the customer will shift from doubt and the need to be persuaded, to wishing to buy.

Any question or statements about money, price or affordability is a buying signal.

The customer will switch from asking questions on *why* they should buy to discussing price and delivery. Customers who are ready to buy may well begin to negotiate on price and terms. They may ask questions to confirm that they have made the right choice. They might ask about other customers' feelings about the product.

Interpret all of these actions as buying signals. In each case go for the close.

Verbal signals

Listen for verbal signals that the customer is ready to buy. The customer's voice will become less hesitant. He will become more positive about the product. He will say something like 'yes' and 'right'.

The customer will use the word 'will' rather than 'might' or 'would'. The customer will start to ask about the best price.

Features and benefits

As they get closer to the purchase decision customers begin to ask more questions about the features and benefits.

If this happens ask which benefits are important to them. Talk about those features that provide the needed benefits.

Questions about quality

If the customer asks questions about quality they are interested.

They want reassurance and confirmation that they are making the right decision. They want you to confirm that they will get good value for money.

Customers may ask questions to benchmark you against a competitor's products. If this happens ask why quality is important to them. Use their answer to sell the benefits.

Ownership questions

Just before deciding to buy the customer will imagine owning the product. He will ask questions about using it.

The customer might ask "Will I need to service this every 9000 miles?" They might ask how long the parts will last or how to operate, maintain or clean the equipment.

At this stage the customer is imagining what it would be like to own the product.

Warranty questions

If the customer asks questions about warranty or guarantees then they are already imagining ownership. They just want you to lessen the risk involved in the purchase. Reassure them and you have the sale.

Problems with previous vendors

If a customer complains about service from a previous vendor they want reassurance that you will look after their needs correctly.

Questions about you and your company

Any questions about you or your company are buying signals. At this stage the customer wants the product. They just want to be sure that you are reliable and trust worthy. If you can persuade them that you represent a reputable firm then you have the sale.

Questions about other customer experiences

The buyer will buy if you tell him that other customers were delighted with the product and the after service.

Questions about the next stage

If the customer has decided to buy the product he will ask questions about the next stage in the process.

The customer will ask about price and finance. The customer will ask about availability. The customer will ask about timescales such as delivery and set up.

The customer's speech may speed up. If you get questions of this sort you can go straight to the assumptive close:

Customer: "Can you deliver next Wednesday?"
Salesperson: "Do you need delivery Wednesday?"
Customer: "Yes."
Salesperson: "OK great, let me arrange that right away."

Questions about after sales service

If the customer asks about after sales service they are ready to buy. They just need reassurance that you will provide excellent after sales service. Just reassure them and go for the close.

Asking for testimonials or a reference

If the customer asks about testimonials or references then they are sold on the product, providing they can trust you and your company. Ask if they would be happy to proceed if you provide the references. Then give several references or testimonials or a list of satisfied customers.

Body language signals

If the customer is ready to buy their body language will become more relaxed. They will switch from looking guarded, sceptical and doubtful to looking interested and positive.

Customers who are ready to buy become less guarded and withdrawn. They begin to look friendly. They might smile and nod their heads. They will appear eager. They will lean in and look to connect with you. They will look at the product and touch it.

Asking you to repeat detail

If a customer asks you to repeat something you said about the offer then they are interested.

If they were not interested they would want you to stop talking as soon as possible so they can escape.

Action signals

Customers will read sales literature and brochures to confirm that they have made the right decision. They might measure the product to make sure that it will fit in their desired location.

They might try the product out, because they cannot wait to get it delivered. They might bring a friend with them on a second visit to help confirm that they have made the right decision.

Chapter 18. Responding to buying signals

Varying customer signals

If you meet customers in a store they will be in one of four states. You must quickly work out which one they are in. Your approach will vary in each stage.

- Just browsing. Killing time, but might be open to impulse buys.
- Interested but not anxious to buy.
- Very interested. Will buy if you can answer the right questions.
- Anxious to buy immediately and leave.

Just browsing

A customer may tell you that they are just browsing. They will avert eye contact. Tell them that you will be glad to assist them if they need any help. Then back off and watch them from a distance.

If they focus in on one product range they probably have some degree of interest. The longer they spend looking at a product the more interested they are. You will have a better chance of selling it to them.

Interested

If they look in your direction you can approach and be available if they ask any questions.

If they continue to look towards you move in closer and ask if they need some help. Begin the sale at this stage.

Very interested

If the customer is very interested they will ask questions about the product. They will touch the product and might pick it up. They may ask a friend for their opinion of the product.

They may have a checklist of features that they want. Find out their needs before talking about the features and the benefits. If they are looking at a range of products and ask about price try to find out their budget. Point out the product that will give them the most benefit or value for their money.

Anxious to buy

If someone is anxious to buy they will look around for a salesperson. They will pick the product up. They will take out their purse or wallet. They will move towards the sales counter.

Just approach this person and ask if you can get that for them. The sale is made.

Do not unmake the sale with unnecessary talk.

Answering questions

The buying signal will often come from the customer in the form of a question as explained in the previous chapter.

Never answer this question with a simple 'yes' or 'no.' Never answer a buying signal question by giving the facts.

You may be asked, "Can you deliver next week?" Never answer with a simple, "Yes."

You may be asked, "How long does it take to deliver?" Never answer with a factual answer such as, "three days."

Instead reply with a question of your own to move to a trial close. So in response to the question above say something like, "When would you like us to deliver?" If the answer is Thursday, then you simply say "No problem. Let me arrange that for you now."

Sample questions and responses

Customer: Do you have this model in red?
Salesperson: Do you want it in red?
Customer: Yes.
Salesperson: I'll get you one now.

Customer: Can you deliver next Tuesday?
Salesperson: Do you want it delivered next Tuesday?
Customer: Yes.
Salesperson: I'll arrange that for you right away.

Customer: Do you have this size in stock?
Salesperson: Do you need this size?
Customer: Yes.
Salesperson: I'll get you one now.

Customer: Does it come with a three-year warranty?
Salesperson: Do you need a three-year warranty?
Customer: Yes.
Salesperson: Let me sort out the paperwork for you. I just need you to sign here.

Customer: When can you deliver?
Salesperson: When do you need it delivered?
Customer: On Tuesday afternoon.
Salesperson: Let me organise the delivery right away.

Chapter 19. Negotiating

Negotiating is a key skill in sales. You will need to negotiate at times to get the sale. You may need to negotiate on issues like price, quantity, delivery, add-ons and service contracts.

Never negotiate early

Prove the value of the product before you begin negotiations.

Do not allow yourself to be drawn into early negotiations. Go through the full process of identifying needs, selling benefits, recognising the buying signals and at least provisionally closing the sale.

Never start to negotiate before you have the agreement to buy.

If you do negotiate earlier, the customer will link the purchase decision to the required terms. This link will make your task much more difficult.

If the customer obviously wants the product then quickly find out his needs. This way you can argue the value of the product during negotiations.

Negotiate with the right person

Make sure that you are negotiating with the right decision maker. Often salespeople make the mistake of negotiating a deal with buyers. They then find that they are called to a second meeting with more senior people within the organization to finalise the deal.

At this second meeting all the concessions from the original negotiations are taken as agreed. They are then asked for further concessions by the more senior decision maker.

Make sure than all of the interested parties are present at negotiations.

Base any concessions on signing an agreement there and then.

Win-win

Negotiations tend to follow a familiar pattern.

The seller will name the price. This will be more than he is willing to concede. The buyer will make an opening offer. This will be less than he is willing to pay. The haggling begins. Eventually a deal is struck somewhere in the middle.

This is the classic win-win situation. Both parties feel that they have gained something from the deal.

If you want to encourage long-term customer relationships then you need a win-win result.

You will want your new customer to feel that he has gotten something from the deal.

You will want an outcome that works for both parties. This is the only result that will lead to a long-term business arrangement. The buyer must feel that he is getting value for money. This is the best way to get him to return for more.

If there is any buyer's remorse then you have sacrificed future business for short-term gain.

Your negotiating strategy

Aim high and allow the customer to negotiate you down.

Work out in advance:

- Your ideal selling package.
- What you are likely to get.
- Your bottom line, which is the minimum you will accept.

Be prepared to walk away if you cannot secure your bottom line agreement.

There is no point making a loss on the deal.

Tailor your package to meet the customer's needs. Stress the benefits of the product. Link the product's worth directly to the value that it brings to the customer.

Know where you can apply some pressure.

The importance of price

Only discount the price as a last resort. Company sales revenue pays everyone's wages. If you discount the price the lost revenue comes straight off the bottom line.

If asked for a discount, stress the quality of the product and the value to the customer. Use one of the following answers if asked about discounts.

- Sorry, but we have a fixed price strategy.
- We cannot afford to let our other customers know that we are selling for less.
- We only offer discount for volume. I can take you through the rates if you like.
- This product is selling at a premium.
- There is a waiting list for this product.
- This product is extremely popular.
- This product has a very low depreciation rate.

Be willing to offer something else rather than a price discount.

Get agreement on all other terms and conditions before negotiating on price. Only discount the price if the buyer is willing to immediately sign a contract.

Negotiate the total package

Negotiate the total package so that you can trade on concessions. This will allow you to avoid discounting the price.

Trade concessions

Never give a concession without getting something in return.

For instance only discount price if the customer agrees to increase the volume of the order.

Have a game plan. Know in advance which concessions you are willing to give. Know the order in which you are willing to trade them. Know what you want in return.

Give a final sweetener.

Always keep a concession to the end. This helps to secure the deal. The customer usually expects one final enticement to sign the contract.

Concessions that you may want to get from the customer

- To buy the most expensive model they can afford.
- To place a bigger order.
- To purchase some add-ons.
- To agree to repeat orders.
- To agree to a long-term commitment.
- To take out your finance package.

- To sign up to your warranty package.

Do not get involved in conflict

While you will want to negotiate as good a deal as possible you must keep the mood light.

It is all right to be firm and to ask for what you want. However do not issue demands and ultimatums. Always remain professional and polite.

Never lock the buyer into a position, he may withdraw his offer.

Do not antagonise the buyer or you could lose him. Do not force him into a corner. You do not want him to become entrenched.

Try to sit alongside the buyer. This is less confrontational. Use a common aid such as a diagram or a sketch. This helps you to cooperate rather than confront each other.

If the buyer becomes entrenched try looking at a different package.

The importance of deadlines

Understand the importance of deadlines.

- At month end the seller may want to close a deal to hit his bonus.
- The seller may need to offload stock because a major order has fallen through.
- Near the end of the financial year the buyer may need to spend or lose the balance of his budget.
- The buyer may need a quick delivery as another supplier has let him down.

All of these examples would lead one party to concede more than they would normally do.

Write out the agreement

Summarise the agreement with the customer at the end of the negotiations.

Write down some bullet points. Tell the customer you will send a letter of agreement the next day. This will ensure there are no misunderstandings.

Buyer's strategy

Buyers will always hint at bigger orders in the future. Just tell the buyer that you will be happy to offer a better deal when you get that bigger order. Only make concessions now if the buyer places the bigger order now for future delivery.

If the buyer hints at a better offer from the competition ask to see the written quotation. It could well be that the other offer is not identical. You may be able to match it by stripping out some of the extras

The buyer may say that his budget has been reduced. If this is a genuine problem look at financing the terms. Alternatively come up with a different package the customer can afford.

Overcoming buyer's anxiety

Some buyers become anxious when asked to sign a large contract. If this is the case just take the buyer through the pros and cons of the deal. Highlight all the advantages to him. Show how these advantages far outweigh any risks involved. Reassure the buyer that you will support him at every stage.

Chapter 20. Closing the sale

Closing

Closing is the final stage in the sales cycle. It involves getting the customer to agree to buy the product.

Choose the right time to close. This is when it is obvious to the customer that your product is the best match for his needs. Do not be tempted to close the sale any earlier than this.

When the customer is ready to buy they will start to send subconscious buying signals. It is up to you to detect these signals and close the sale.

If you have followed all the stages of the sales cycle correctly the customer will want to buy. They should only need a little encouragement.

Ask for the sale

> *You must ask, if you want to make the sale.*

More important than this, you must ask at the right time.

You would be surprised at the number of salespeople who do not ask for the sale and so do not get the business.

> *Ask and you shall receive.*

Closing the sale involves asking a question, the answer to which confirms the sale.

Do not give them the option of saying no

When asking for the sale, do not give the customer the chance to say '*no*.' Never ask a question like, "Would you like me to place the order?" This gives the customer the opportunity to answer, "No."

Use a preference question instead, such as, "Would you prefer the standard or the four wheel drive model?"

You could also use a time based question such as, "Would you like delivery this week or next week?"

Do not become tense

Do not become tense when you try to close the sale. The customer will detect any changes to your body language and tone of voice. This will cause them to doubt your sincerity. They will back away from the sale.

Just remain calm. Smile and keep your body language warm, friendly and open.

Earn the right

You cannot close the sale until you have earned the right. This involves finding out the customer's needs, meeting theses needs, overcoming objections and building rapport. All the while you guide the customer towards the close.

If you try to close before carrying out these preparatory steps you will get an objection or a simple 'No'.

Keep the endgame in mind

Every step you take should be building up to closing the sale.

Focus your efforts in moving in that direction. Always assume that you will get the sale. Get agreement at each stage before you move on to the next step.

You cannot skip any steps unless the customer is sending you buying signals.

Trial close

If a client gives off buying signals go for the trial close.

The trial close allows you to read the buyer's position. It reveals how close they are to making the buying decision. Just ask a question to attempt the close.

If you have misread the signals the customer may give an objection or simply stall. This is fine. You answer the objection or continue with the sales pitch.

Always get confirmation to continue at each stage of the sales cycle. If you get a "maybe" or "I'm not sure," you need to probe deeper. You need to get to the real objection before continuing.

Asking questions

Ask questions to lead the customer towards a close. Ask if your product meets each of his specified needs. Each time the customer confirms with a 'yes' you are leading him nearer to the closure.

Make it easy for them to say yes

Help your customer to say yes. Help by accepting finance payments. Take a deposit to secure the sale. Fill in the paperwork for the customer and just ask for their signature.

Sell them value

Customers always want value for money. Find out their needs and sell the features that meet these needs. Point out any extra value your product has compared with the competition. Perhaps the product has been improved recently without any increase in price. Maybe you can offer free after sales service for the first six months.

Do not sell logic

People buy more often based on emotions than logic.

Do not focus your presentation on logical reasons for buying. Apeal to people's emotions if you want to close sales. Focus on the customer's wants rather than their needs.

People buy a lot more goods because they want them, rather than strictly needing them.

Concentrate on the emotional reasons for buying

People buy products because they want them. People want products for mainly emotional reasons. Often the reason is status, pride, prestige or ego. If their neighbour gets a brand-new car, then they want one also. Teenagers follow fashion trends for the same reasons. They want to belong.

People will also buy for reasons of health and security. Insurance salespeople use stories of people who suffered terrible losses and who were not properly insured. This method appeals to the fear of loss. It also appeals to the need to provide security to family and loved ones.

Under promise

Never promise anything you cannot deliver. It is better to under promise. Perhaps your average delivery is six weeks from order.

Just tell the customer the delivery cycle can take from six to nine weeks. Then promise to do what you can.

Over deliver

If you deliver an order sooner that promised the customer will believe that you care about them and will look after their needs.

The importance of silence

You must understand the importance of silence.

When you ask for the sale you must remain silent until you get the answer.

Keep quiet when you ask for the sale. Do not prompt the other person. Do not try to influence their answer. Do not open your mouth. Say nothing until the prospect answers.

If you speak first you will lose the sale.

If they agree say as little as possible until they have signed the contract. You do not want to feed any doubts that they may have.

Sell the add-ons

Once you have sold the main product sell the add-ons. Do not say, "Will there be anything else?" The customer will always answer, "No."

If you sell a suit show the customer a suitable shirt and tie. If you sell a major piece of equipment sell the maintenance contract or extended warranty with it.

Do not pack up until you have closed the sale

Never pack up your equipment until after you have closed the sale. You have taken twenty minutes to get their attention and build up the emotional attachment.

Strike while the iron is hot.

If you pack up after you give the presentation and then try to close the sale you will probably lose the sale. Your audience will have switched off mentally. They will lose the emotional attachment you have built up. They will begin to think about the other urgent matters that they need to deal with. Your chance will have gone.

After the sale

Do not just rush out the door once you have closed the sale. First thank the customer for his business. Then assure him that:

- He has made the right decision.
- You will deliver on your promises.
- You value them as a customer.
- You are looking forward to doing business with them.
- You will make sure the order is delivered on time.
- You will ring once they have received delivery to make sure that they are happy.

Give the customer your contact details. Tell them to ring you if they have any queries or problems. Explain the next steps in the process. Give them the contact details of your customer services department.

When you next contact the customer, make sure that buyer's remorse has not set in.

Then answer any genuine concerns the customer has. Reassure them that they have made the right decision. This will avoid a cancellation, return and a lost customer.

The customer needs to be satisfied with the goods.

Satisfied customers return for more.

Get the referral

Once you have the sale make sure that you get the referral. Ask for the names of someone they know who would be interested in your product also.

Record what worked

Afterwards, make a record of what helped you to close a sale. You can repeat these techniques with new prospects.

Send a thank you card

If you get new business from a customer send them a thank you card. Follow up every visit to a customer with an email or letter. Thank them for their time and their hospitality.

Chapter 21. Closing techniques

Before applying closing techniques

The average prospect will say 'no' five times before they say yes. Do not let a negative response put you off. Influence the customer to say 'yes.' Know how to employ various closing techniques.

You need to know more closing techniques than the average buyer has objections.

This way you can bridge from one failed closing attempt to another. Just listen to and deal with the objection. Clarify that there are no further objections and go for the close again using an alternative technique.

Never employ a closing technique until you have received enough buying signals.

Several techniques are listed below. Only employ them when the time and circumstances are right. You must work through each stage of the sales cycle unless you receive buying signals early on. Concentrate on building rapport and a relationship with the customer.

No amount of closing techniques can substitute for properly following the stages of the sales cycle. You need to lead the customer to the sale by asking the right questions.

If the customer feels that you are pushing them into a sale they will walk away.

People do not return to pushy salespeople. People do not like being sold to. They recognise closing techniques for what they are. Only use closing techniques when the customer is close to making the buying decision. Wait until they only needs a little persuasion.

Before employing these techniques:

- Ask questions to establish needs.
- Listen carefully.
- Focus on the customer's needs.
- Be seen to be helping rather than selling.
- Focus on the benefits to the client.
- Establish their budget.
- Offer a limited choice of two options.
- Offer the cheapest product first, below their budget, to establish trust.
- Give the customer time to consider and discuss his options.
- Deal with any objections.
- Remain positive throughout.
- Reassure the customer that he is making the right choice.

Technique 1-2-3

Summarise the offer in sets of three items. I can give you that price, with these benefits and these add-ons.

You can offer something on price, specification and timing. Alternatively you can compare your product on all three items. For example you could say, "Our product is cheaper, it lasts longer and we can deliver three weeks sooner than anyone else."

Combining three things leads the client to believe that they are getting a once-off bargain. They will be more inclined to accept the offer.

Make the offer affordable

Find out what the buyer can afford and then tailor a package to suit. Strip out extras that they do not need. Get a finance plan that they can meet. Talk about payback savings. Show them how it will cost more to maintain their old product in the long run.

The alternative close

The alternative close does not give the buyer the option of refusing.

Give them the choice of two options, either of which gets you the sale.

An example would be, "Would you like a delivery on the second or third week in July?"

The client usually opts for the second option. It is the last thing they hear and so easier to recall. Use this to your advantage by stating your preferred option last.

For example, "Will I put you down for the two year finance package or the three year deal?" An alternative might be, "Would you like our standard option or our additional value package?"

In both cases the second option provides more revenue and profit.

The artisan close

This closure technique is used to improve the perceived quality of the product. The customer feels that they are getting better value for money.

You could emphasise the art, skill and craft that went in to making the product

Ask-the-manager close

Some customers love to haggle. When the discount they demand is getting close to your bottom line say that you are not authorised to give any more discount. Say that you need to discuss any further discount with the manager. Go off and stand at the open doorway to a nearby office. The customer will see and hear you remonstrating on their behalf.

The technique works better if the manager 'berates' you for being a soft touch. When he finally relents you return with an extra 5% discount.

The customer is impressed that you have fought on their behalf. They feel that they should reciprocate. The sale is then closed.

The assumptive close

With this method you act as if the deal is agreed. You ask a question to imply this. You could say something like, "When do you need me to deliver?"

The technique works because the customer wants to avoid confrontation. They do not want to point out that you are wrong in your assumption. You are effectively not giving the client a chance to back out.

If the customer does give an objection then just ask if that is the only problem. Answer the objection and then close the sale.

The balance sheet close

With the balance sheet close you list the pros and cons of the offer. The cons might be where your product is missing some features. You give a shortlist of minor cons and then give a long list of major pros. By doing this you are seen to be honest and objective. Yet you are guiding their thinking.

The customer can obviously see that the pros outweigh the cons. They conclude that the offer is a good one. You can use your tone of voice to emphasise the pros. You should sound delighted that you can include these.

The bonus close

The bonus close is where you add an unexpected extra or bonus to close the sale. This technique can be used with customers on the verge of agreement.

The bonus close works because the customer wants to complete the deal before you decide to withdraw the bonus.

The bracket close

The bracket close works by showing the customer a top of the range product, beyond his budget. You then show the base product that does not meet his needs. Finally you offer a mid-priced product that meets all his needs and wants.

The customer sees the choice as being easy. They feel that they have gotten value for money. They have saved on the additional cost of the expensive product. By rejecting the cheap item they position themselves above those people who cannot afford better.

The calculator close

As the name suggests you take out a large calculator and tell the customer that you want to work out the best price for him.

Key in the full price and talk the customer through the deductions. Take your time. Deliberately give the impression of having to make difficult decisions. Say something like, "The ticket price is £1500. We have a 10% discount deal this week, so that makes £1350. Let me see. What's the best I can do for you today? How about I take off another £100 and make it £1250 for you?"

This technique works because you are working out a special price for the customer. By working it out and showing the results to the customer you are finalising the deal. The customer will be reluctant to ask you to recalculate.

This technique is often used with high ticket price items such as jewellery.

The companion close

The companion close works well in the retail environment. Take an example where a young couple is shopping in a store. The man asks to try on a jacket. When he does you concentrate on his lady companion.

You compliment the jacket. Ask the lady if she thinks that it looks well on her partner. Talk about how good the fit looks. Get her to agree again. Return to the young man and ask him if he is happy with the jacket. At this stage he is more inclined to agree. After all both you and his partner have confirmed the choice.

The companion does not have to make the financial commitment and so they are more likely to agree with you.

This technique works because it is easier to get the agreement of the companion. The buyer concedes as he does not want to contradict his companion.

The concession close

With this method the salesperson offers a final concession on condition that the customer will agree to buy. It is similar to the bonus close. The difference is that you make it clear the concession is a one-off offer. It is based on closing the sale today.

The cost of ownership close

The cost of ownership close is used when the product is expensive. The total up-front cost may be causing reluctance with the customer. You can also use it when you have a high quality product that is more expensive than your competitors.

An example would be how Fairy Liquid is advertised as lasting so much longer than the competitor products. Therefore the product offers the best value for money.

With this approach you could point out that:

- Your product lasts longer.
- It is cheaper to insure.
- It has lower running costs.
- It has much lower maintenance costs.
- It has lower depreciation and so will fetch a much better trade in price.

Have a printed comparison drawn up between your product and the main competitor's equivalent product. This calculates the total monthly cost of ownership alongside the competitor's product that at first seems to be less expensive. This shows how your product is better value for money over the lifetime of the product.

The daily cost close

In this case the cost is expressed at a daily rate rather than an annual rate.

This method is often used for rental costs such as mobile phone or insurance costs. The person selling will say something like, "This package offers great value at only 79 pence per day." This is much better than saying it costs £289 per year.

Often the customer is unable to calculate the annual cost. They simply consider the daily cost as being good value for money.

The demonstration close

This works well if the product is novel or its performance exceeds normal expectations. This method is often used for children's or adult toys such as remote control cars or helicopters.

Let the customer try out the product. This gets them emotionally attached. It builds the desire to own the product.

As a crowd gathers you also get the effect of the herd instinct. If one customer asks to buy the product, more will follow suit.

The diagram close

With the diagram close you sit alongside the customer with a blank sheet of paper. You then draw a diagram of some aspect of your product while explaining the process.

The advantage to this method is that you are not sitting opposite in an adversarial position.

By employing this method you are taking the time to explain in detail the benefits of the system. You are leading the customer one step at a time. The customer cannot get ahead of you as you have not finished the drawing yet.

The visual impact ensures that you grab the customer's curiosity. It keeps their attention as you outline your points. You can draw schematics and graphs to show how savings can be made or how revenues will accrue.

The economic close

This method works well with a customer who is considering buying a product. You point out an alternative that offers better value for money. By doing so, you can often increase the overall revenue that you take.

You can point out, for example, that the family pack is much better value for money. You could remind the customer that if they buy three they can get one free.

This approach builds trust as you are offering to save the customer money.

Embarrassment close

The embarrassment close involves showing the customer the cheapest product. You then demonstrate a more expensive product that you want to sell to them.

Tell the customer that you feel the second product would suit their budget better as it has certain benefits.

This approach is often used with young men accompanied by their spouses.

No one wants to be perceived as a cheapskate.

The empathy close

With the empathy close you show empathy for the customer's concerns.

Perhaps the customer expresses concern about the product breaking down. You could say that you have bought the product and found it to be excellent and reliable. In addition you have not had any returns on this product which has been selling for the last year.

By displaying empathy and concern for the candidate you are building trust. You are making it easier for them to make the decision.

The exclusivity close

With this method you seem to exclude the customer from a special offer. You then find a way to include them in the offer.

You could say that a discount is for members only. No one likes to be excluded. They want to be a member of an exclusive club.

The customer will want the extra discount. They will ask if there is any way that you can provide it. You then relent and say that you can sign them up as a new member.

The fire sale close

Fire sales are discount offers not to be repeated, such as bankrupt or returned stock. You can close the sale by saying that this is the last model in stock.

The customer buys because they know that they are getting a price that will not be repeated. They are essentially getting a new product for second hand prices.

The give-take close

This method is also known as the negative sale. With this method you offer the customer something. You then immediately withdraw the offer. This arouses the customer's desire for the product.

For example you could offer a table to the customer. You then remember that another customer has reserved the product by placing a deposit on it.

The customer will ask if there is anything you can do. Say that you will check the order book. Then say that the other customer wanted delivery next week. You can let the customer have this table now. You will get on to your suppliers and ask them to fast track delivery for the initial customer. It might cost you a little more, but you are happy to do this to help the customer out.

This method takes advantage of the scarcity principle. The product is obviously desirable if another customer has placed a deposit. You also enable the customer to regain lost control over the process. The customer feels that they have won.

The guilt close

The guilt close implies that the customer's current product does not conform to the social trends. For example you could say that everyone is now buying the eco-friendly model.

The guilt close can also imply that the customer will appear to be mean by not buying an item. For example you could say, "All the other parents are buying these trainers."

The handshake close

This method is often used after haggling a little on price. If you are nearing your bottom line extend your hand and ask for the deal. Smile and nod and perhaps raise your eyebrows. The other person will feel obliged to shake hands on the deal.

The no hassle close

With this method you make it easy for the customer. For example you could say, "Do not worry sir we can deliver, install and set up this product free of charge any day you want. I can sort out the paperwork for you. I just need your signature."

This method removes any anticipated difficulty in the buyer's mind. It removes any unspoken objections. It makes the transaction hassle free.

The once off offer

The once off is an offer that you will not be repeated.

With this method you could point out that this is the last day of the sale. Remaining stock is limited. The current offer will not hold tomorrow.

The customer is forced to make a decision without the time to look at alternatives elsewhere.

The opportunity cost close

With the opportunity cost close you point out the cost of not taking action.

For example you could point out the added maintenance costs on their older equipment.

You could sell a Health and Safety course for team leaders using this method. Point out the cost of not investing in training and proper safety procedures. This would involve the cost of the lost hours at work due to accidents, the overtime needed to cover this absence, the cost of settling claims for compensation and added insurance costs.

The ownership close

With the ownership close you paint a mental picture in the customer's mind of them owning the product. You talk and act as if they already own the product.

For example you could say something like, "I think your friends and family will really like your new kitchen table."

By employing this technique you are associating the customer with the product and thus helping him to make the buying decision.

The price promise

With the price promise you offer to refund the difference if the customer can get the product anywhere locally cheaper. Tell the customer that you know most people like to shop around. However, you can save them all that time and effort. You can guarantee that you offer the best price.

Set a time limit on the offer. Your product may be cheaper at the moment. However it will not remain cheaper if your competitor includes their offering in a sale.

The technique eliminates the customer's fear that your product is not the cheapest available. You will get a few customers claiming the difference. However, most customers do not bother to do so.

The puppy dog close

Imagine if you let a couple with young children take a puppy dog home on a trial basis to see how they like it before deciding to buy. Just think of the pressure those parents will be under from the kids to keep that puppy.

The puppy dog close involves a free trial membership or ownership. The customer is given the option to return the product if they are not 100% satisfied.

Test-driving a car is a form of puppy dog close. The theory is that once you get to touch and experience the car it will almost sell itself. Your mind will make subconscious favourable comparisons with your current model.

The quality close

With this approach you emphasise the quality of the product. You show how it will perform better, last longer, need less maintenance and depreciate less over time. This shows how the product represents value for money.

You can also relate the quality to the customer's feeling of self-image. For instance you could say, "Discerning customers usually choose this product." Or you could say, "We have an elite clientele who usually ask for this package." This method appeals to their sense of vanity.

The rational close

Most people's buying decisions are determined by emotion. However there are still some customers who use a logical approach to decision making.

With this type of customer you can stress the scientific proof that confirms that the product performs as promised. Most people believe in scientific proof. Point out how the product meets all of their needs and is the logical choice for them.

The repetition close

With the repetition close you show the customer the product you want to sell. You then show them other products one at a time and mention their disadvantages.

Each time you mention the disadvantage of an alternative product you point out a benefit of the product that you want to sell. Hand it back to the customer each time to point out the feature.

After three or four repetitions you will have overcome any doubts. You will have persuaded the customer that this is the best choice for them.

The requirements close

With this technique you ask the customer for all of his requirements.

Simply write down all of the customer's needs in turn. Then ask if you have all the requirements. If not, you add to the list. Get the customer to confirm that you have written down all of his requirements.

Now ask if you can get the sale if you can meet all of these needs. When the customer confirms go through the requirements one at a time. Show how your offering meets the needs in each case.

The sharp angle close

The sharp angle close is based on the porcupine technique of answering a question with another question.

For example the customer might say, "Can you deliver next Wednesday." You resist the temptation to say yes and instead answer with, "Do you need delivery next Wednesday?"
You remain silent until the customer confirms. Then you say "Let me arrange that for you."

The similarity close

With this method you mention a similar customer who had the same objection but was delighted with the product.

You overcome the objection by showing empathy. The customer is obviously reasonable in their objection as someone else felt the same way.

You then persuade them that their fear is unfounded. Tell the story of a similar customer who was more than satisfied with their purchase.

The summary close

With this method you close by summarising all the benefits the customer has already agreed on.

The testimonial close

If you are selling a high value item such as double glazing or a fitted kitchen you can show written testimonials. You can offer to take the customer to see a job you have already installed.

The customer who has agreed to act as a referee will have received a discount. This will have been in return for agreeing to allow a given number of prospective customers to view the installation.

The testimonial close reassures the prospective customer about the quality of the finish.

The think about it close

If you are selling an expensive item you might want the customer to try out the product and think about it. By allowing them to touch and experience the product you ensure that they form an emotional attachment to it.

You only make this offer after you have identified their needs and listed the benefits that meet these.

You could then suggest the customer takes a little time to think about the decision. You could say something like, "Would you like to sit in this showroom model and think about this."

The treat close

With this method you tell the customer that they deserve a treat.

You would use this approach if the customer says, "I do not know if I should spend so much on myself."

Your response would be "Go ahead and treat yourself. You deserve it."

The valuable customer close

With this method you offer a one-off discount because you value their custom.

This technique flatters the customer by making a unique offer based on their status.

You could offer to install a conservatory at a discounted rate as the customer is buying a large prestige model. In return you would like to include some photographs of the installed conservatory in your next brochure. The offer appeals to the customer's ego.

The yes set close

The yes set close is based on asking a series of questions to which the answer is always going to be yes.

This technique conditions the customer to agreeing and saying yes each time.

Get the results that you want by asking leading questions and nodding your head when you want them to say yes.

Chapter 22. When things go wrong

Always look on the bright side of life

Eric Idle summed it up perfectly with his advice to always look on the bright side.

Sometimes you will go through every stage of the sales cycle only to find out there is a problem when it comes to the closing stage.

This can happen if the prospect has not answered your questions truthfully at the earlier stages. Perhaps they do not have the authority to buy as previously claimed.

You can salvage something from every shipwreck.

Look for opportunity in all misfortune. Never surrender at the first set back. Always seek out the opportunity, no matter how limited it may be. The least you should walk away with are some referrals. You will also gain the experience to avoid the situation recurring.

Problems can occur because of the issues outlined below.

Limited budget or authority

The client may have a limited budget or limited authority to buy. They may have been reluctant to admit this earlier.

One option is to arrange to meet with the person with the right authority. The other option is to risk waiting until the initial contact can get extra funding released.

It is much better to complete the deal with the initial contact. You may lose the sale if referred to someone else higher up the chain of command.

Try coming up with a suitable finance package. Alternatively you could repackage the offering by stripping out some features. As a final resort you could discount the price to place the product within the customer's budget.

Only offer discount if it means opening a new account with the definite prospect of repeat business.

The benefits do not match the customer's needs

Perhaps the customer did not answer your questions correctly at the needs analysis stage. This will have caused you to build your presentation around the wrong benefits.

If this is the case ask some probing questions to find out exactly what the client needs and wants. Then change your recommendation based on the newly identified needs. Point out the added features and benefits that meet these needs.

The timing is wrong

There may be several reasons why the timing is wrong. Perhaps the budget is spent. Perhaps the customer is overstocked. Perhaps they are undergoing refurbishments and cannot use your products this month.

Whatever the reason, book a repeat meeting for when circumstances will have improved.

Better still take the order now, for delayed delivery and delayed invoicing.

Chapter 23. Mistakes to avoid

Taking rejection personally

Never take rejection personally. This adds to a feeling of low self-esteem. It leads to a tendency to avoid repetition. This reduces your conversion rates.

> *Rejection is a natural part of the process.*

No matter how skilled you are a certain percentage of customers will always say 'No.' The important thing to do is find out exactly why the customer cannot or will not commit at any given stage.

> *Learn from your failures.*

Look at what went wrong. Work out how you can avoid the situation next time. Do you need to alter your techniques? Perhaps you can return to the customer when circumstances change? Perhaps you can recommend an upgrade to your product?

Regularly analyse your conversation rates. If you have a low conversion rate at any stage of the sales cycle, take the appropriate corrective action.

Not being prepared

Be prepared for every encounter with customers.

> *Fail to prepare and you prepare to fail.*

Performance is directly linked to the level and quality of your planning and preparation.

Talking too much

The biggest mistake you can make as a salesperson is to talk too much. You learn nothing while you are talking.

You do need to ask the right questions to establish needs and objections. You will also have to talk during your pitch and to close. However the customer should be talking twice as much as you are.

Not listening

Your job is to listen carefully, observe body language, take notes, persuade the customer and lead them to the sale.

If you do not listen properly you will not find out the customer's needs. You will also miss the buying signals.

If you do not look at the customer when they are talking they will assume that you are not listening.

Interrupting the customer

Never interrupt the customer. It is discourteous. It reinforces the stereotypical image of the pushy salesperson.

Not establishing needs

If you do not establish the needs correctly, then you will sell the wrong benefits.

Not matching benefits to the customer's needs

Once you have established the needs you must sell the associated benefits.

It is a mistake to cover all the features if some of them are not needed by the customer. They will switch off if you talk about features that they do not need. Worse still they will think that they are paying for something that they do not need.

Stick to what is relevant to the customer.

Confusing the customer

If you become too technical, or talk too much, you will confuse the customer. If you offer too many choices you will confuse the customer. If you ask long complicated questions you will confuse the customer.

Confused customers don't buy.

Confused customers become frustrated, embarrassed and flustered. Confused customers leave and go elsewhere. They find someone else who will explain things in a way that they can understand. They buy from people who keep things simple and relate to their individual needs.

Making assumptions

Making assumptions about the customer's needs or wants will cause you to present the wrong benefits. Act on established facts, not assumed opinions.

Not qualifying correctly

Failure to qualify correctly can cause some salespeople to waste time and effort. Do not waste time on people who do not have the ability or authority to buy.

Topping

Never top your customer with a better story.

If the customer tells you how he caught a 6 pound salmon, then do not tell him about the time that you caught an 8 pound salmon.

Always praise the customer's achievements while down playing your own prowess.

Never ever talk down to a customer. They will walk away every time.

Arguing with the customer

Never, ever argue with a customer, especially when he is wrong. If you want the business, then the customer is always right.

> ***You may win the argument, but you will lose the sale.***

If there is a danger of the conversation becoming confrontational, then change the subject and lighten the mood. Never, ever take an opposing stance to the customer.

Using the wrong words

Avoid jargon and technical terms. Stick to describing benefits in simple terms the customer can understand.

Do not say anything that will invoke negative doubts in the customer's mind. Never use negative terms when discussing the product, the competition or anything else.

> ***The customer must be in a positive frame of mind if you are to close a sale.***

Any negative connotations will cause the customer to reject the offering.

Not closing at the right time

Usually you will not get the sale unless you ask for it.

However it is a mistake to try to close too early, before going through the necessary stages of the sales cycle.

It is also a mistake to close too late. You must recognise the buying signals and act on them immediately by asking a question that closes the sale. If you keep talking you may say something that sews doubt in the customer's mind.

Not knowing how to close the sale

There are scores of methods for closing the sale. Learn these techniques and apply one or more of these in every sales encounter. You should know which closing technique will work best in any given situation.

Not being sincere

Not being sincere will lose the sale every time.

The customer must feel that you are there to help and serve them. You must be providing a service that is of benefit to them. It must not appear that your only interest is to get the commission. You must be genuinely interested in serving the customer and satisfying their needs

If you sell a customer something that they do not want or need you will be viewed as a con man. They will tell dozens of other potential customers of their bad experience and this will lead to lost business.

Criticising the competition

It is OK to point out objectively how your products are superior to the competition. It is a different matter to criticise them, particularly in a negative or personal way.

Never talk badly about the competition.

Confirm that the competition is good in certain areas, but point out the areas where your product is superior.

Bad-mouthing the competition is usually frowned on by customers.

Bear in mind that the customer may have had a relationship with the competition for some time. By being critical of the competition you are questioning the customer's judgement.

Not answering objections effectively

You must be able to answer all objections effectively.

Check with the customer at each stage that you have answered these objections to their satisfaction. You cannot continue until you have answered the objections.

Not asking for referrals

Every time you meet a new prospect aim to get three referrals at the end of the meeting.

Ask for referrals regardless of the outcome of the meeting.

Too many sale people make the mistake of not asking for these referrals. Referrals generate business.

Not providing the after service

If you do not provide excellent after sales service then the customer will eventually go elsewhere.

It is the little things that count.

Follow up on every order you take to make sure that it is delivered on time. Ask the customer if they are happy with the product after it is delivered. Keep in regular contact with the customer. Keep the customer updated on product developments. Answer all customer queries promptly. Provide an excellent after sales service.

Take care of your customers or someone else will take care of them for you.

Not spending time with the customer

If you want to keep a customer then you need to become friends. If you want to become friends then you need to spend time with them.

You need to spend time with customers to build rapport.

Never simply give a customer a pair of tickets for the theatre or sporting event. It is much better to go with them.

Being too anxious to get the sale

Appearing over anxious to get the sale will lose the sale. So also will appearing more interested in your commission or your priorities.

If a customer detects anxiety it sews doubt in their mind. The customer will assume that you are hiding something from them.

Pressurising the customer

No one wants to be sold to. If you apply too much pressure, too soon you will scare the customer off.

You must be non threatening to the customer. Refrain from manipulating the customer in any way. You should guide the customer subtly towards the sale. The customer should feel that they are making the choice of their own free will.

Poor time management

Proper time management is critical in any sales career.

Continually generate and follow up on enough leads to provide sufficient sales revenue each month. To do this you must manage your time effectively each and every day.

Chapter 24. Overcome setbacks

Setbacks are inevitable

If you are going to work in the sales profession then you are going to get setbacks. Setbacks are inevitable.

The most common setback is rejection.

People will slam doors in your face. They will hang up the phone on you. They will walk straight on by when you approach with your carefully rehearsed pitch. You will hear the word 'no' much more often than you ever hear the word 'yes'.

Rejection is an integral part of the process. You must learn to treat it as such. You will not be able to close every sale. You will not always have the right products for the customer. The customer will not always be ready to buy.

Selling is a percentage game.

It is up to you to improve the odds in your favour, but you will not win every time.

You can minimise the losses through proper planning and preparation. However, you will not be able to eliminate them completely.

Learn to be philosophical and accept that rejection is a part of the game.

If you cannot eliminate rejection and other setbacks, then learn to deal with them.

The most basic human emotion is the need for acceptance. People do not want to be rejected and cast aside. They want to belong. You will need to overcome this natural *emotional* reaction to rejection. You will have to replace this with the *logical* acceptance of the odds stacked against you.

You are in control

When dealing with setbacks, the most important thing to do is accept that you are still in control. What happens to you is not the important thing.

> ***It is how you respond to setbacks that matters.***

You cannot always persuade the customer to take the action you want. However you can control how you react to every situation.

You are free to choose how you respond to rejection. No one is forcing you to behave in a given manner. If you capitulate and adapt a defeatist reaction, then you only have yourself to blame. You control your actions and reactions. It is up to you how you respond.

Salvage what you can

Your behaviour can make a bad situation worse or it can salvage some good from the setback.

> ***Do not burn your bridges.***

Act graciously when you fail to close a sale. Get what you can from the situation. Continue to display empathy with the customer. Ask for a referral. Ask to call back in a few weeks to see if the situation has changed. Ask what you can do to further satisfy the customer's needs.

Do not be too anxious or disappointed when you fail to close the sale. Just because a customer rejects a proposal today, it does not mean the situation will be the same next month.

Persevere

It can take 6 or 7 follow up visits to get to an agreement to buy. At each stage your goal is to move to the next stage of the sales cycle.

If you have qualified the prospect correctly and they have the ability and authority to buy, then you should persevere.

Concentrate your resources where you are most likely to make the sale. However do not give up on anyone at an earlier stage of the sales cycle.

Persistence is the secret to sales success.

If you give up too early a competitor will come in and poach your prospect.

Understand the importance of failure

Failure is not a terminal situation, unless you allow it to become so.

Treat all failure as an intermittent step.

Treat failure as an opportunity to learn something new.

The most successful people in any walk of life fail the most.

Successful people fail the most because they try the most. They are prepared to risk more than anyone else. They are prepared to put in twice the effort. They are willing to set higher targets. They know that by doing so they will miss some targets. However this does not discourage them. They stick to their goals.

Successful people also learn the most from their mistakes. They analyse what happened and decide on where they went wrong. They understand what did not work. They know what not to try next time.

The road to success is paved with failure.

For a successful person failure is merely a preparation step on the road to success. The more they fall down, the quicker they learn to get straight back up again and carry on.

Every time you try to make a sale you expose yourself to the possibility of failure. However you also have an equal possibility of winning.

To win you must take part in the game.

The more you play, the more experienced you become and the more often you will win. It is as simple as that.

The person who never made a mistake, never made anything.

If you want to avoid rejection completely then you will be unable to act.

Every action involves the risk of failure. The important thing is to understand what went wrong and the underlying cause. You then simply alter your approach the next time.

Do not take it personally

You must not take rejection personally.

Do not equate rejection with your self-worth.

Rejection is simply the undesired result from carrying out a given action under a given set of circumstances. Rejection is not the outcome you expected or wanted. Nevertheless, it is just an outcome.

Treat rejection like the results of an experiment.

The outcome of the experiment was predetermined by the input and the particular circumstances. Either the input was not correct or you misread the circumstances. What you need to do is repeat the experiment. Next time use a different input, or alter the circumstances. It is a process of trial and elimination. You will find the winning formula if you carry out enough experiments.

Understand the meaning of 'No'

Rejection is not a sign of your self-worth. The customer is refusing the product or service, not you as a person.

In addition, the customer is only refusing the product at this particular time. If his circumstances change he may later accept the product.

Keep a database of all your refusals. Return to these customers every three months with your latest offering.

Learn to deal with setbacks while keeping your overall goals firmly in sight. You must be willing to prevail. You must have the desire to win and a belief in your abilities. Develop the will to continue even when the odds seem firmly stacked against you.

Listen to feedback

Ask for and listen to feedback from customers. Try to get them to be both *objective* and *specific* in their feedback. Ask a few probing questions to achieve this. If they are reluctant to broach the issue with you directly then get your boss to ring up and ask why. Learn from the feedback.

Once you know what went wrong you are half way to fixing it.

Feedback may not always be positive. It will, however, help you to improve your future performance.

Rejection is just another form of feedback. It is instructive.

React positively to rejection. Welcome all criticism of the product, service or even your own behaviour. Criticism is a clear pointer to how you should improve next time.

Welcome all criticism as an opportunity to improve.

You may receive criticism from your boss. This feedback pinpoints what is holding you back from promotion. Make sure that you let your boss know that you have learned from the experience. Show that you have adapted a better method of behaving.

Strategies for dealing with failure

- Recognise failure as an unavoidable part of the process.
- Do not take rejection personally.
- Learn from every setback.
- Have a set of contingency plans.
- Always remain positive.
- Keep things in context.
- Welcome constructive feedback and criticism.
- Learn from every situation.
- Alter your approach if you do not get the results you expected.
- Never let failure limit your ambitions.
- Never let failure dictate your attitude.

Do not let fear limit your actions

The natural reaction to rejection is to avoid it happening again. The easiest way to do this is to limit the contact in similar situations. Some people will avoid the situation recurring at all costs.

Rejection often comes at the cold calling stage of the sales cycle. Many salespeople do not like making that cold call. They get anxious in anticipation of it.

However, if you are going to be successful you must overcome this anxiety. You need to make those calls. Make the calls early in the day. You will feel relieved that you have got it behind you.

Remain positive

Always strive to keep a positive attitude. Always keep the result in mind. This helps you to keep things in perspective. You will learn to accept setbacks. You will stay focused on your goals.

Think about performance goals, as well as outcome goals. So if you need to make 20 calls each day to get five meetings with prospects, then that is what it takes. The important thing is that you make the 20 calls and focus on the five positive outcomes. The fifteen rejections were just a necessary part of the process.

Positive thinking improves your well-being

Keep a positive and enthusiastic attitude. Do not let negative, self-limiting doubts creep into your mind. Positive thinking improves self-belief. It improves your well-being. It reduces stress. It increases your resilience.

Positive thinking leads to enthusiastic behaviour. Enthusiasm rubs off on others. Enthusiasm attracts customers to your cause. By keeping a positive attitude you are much more likely to succeed.

Challenge that negative inner voice

Self-doubt is the biggest contributor to failure in any career. Self-doubt prevents people from approaching their true potential.

Always concentrate on the facts and not your fears.

Most of our fears and worries are completely unfounded. There is no substance to them.

We suffer from negative conditioning

People are born positive and conditioned by life's experiences to become negative. As children we are conditioned by parents and teachers to believe that we are not as good as we think we are. We are advised to play it safe. We are told not to take risks. We are told that we will harm ourselves. We are wrapped in cotton wool. We are taught how to stay in the comfort zone.

Children adapt the fears and constraints imposed upon them by parents, other adults and older siblings. All of this conditioning limits us from reaching our true potential.

Our judgement is clouded by bias

Most of our self-limiting beliefs are *not* based on facts or objective truths. They are based on preconceived ideas and assumptions. We jump to conclusions based on a limited view of the facts or data available.

The problem is that once we take a stance, our brain is conditioned to only take notice of further supporting data. It ignores any conflicting data as being wrong. This reflexive loop causes our mind to stick with the self-limiting belief. This happens even when there is overwhelming evidence to the contrary.

The danger of self-doubt

Life's negative conditioning and experiences of failure, lead to self-doubt.

Self-doubt is the biggest cause of failure.

If you doubt your own ability you exaggerate the obstacles in your way. You make excuses for not taking the necessary action. You begin to procrastinate. You delay making calls. You delay making appointments. You miss targets.

How often have you dreaded an encounter, only to find out that it was not as daunting as you first feared? You then wonder what all the fuss was about.

Most of our fears are a figment of our own imagination. They result from negative conditioning. Fear is the limit that we set on our own development.

Next time you are concerned about a situation, challenge that negative inner voice. Do not procrastinate. Go ahead and take action. Winning is often a matter of self-belief.

The cost of self-limiting beliefs

Be aware of any self-limiting beliefs. Perhaps you dread cold calling because you fear the negative reaction you will get when you interrupt people.

Think about the affect this self-limiting belief is having on your performance. Perhaps you are not making enough cold calls to meet your sales targets at the end of each month.

Now think rationally about adapting a positive belief instead. Why not concentrate on the fact that you are helping people by providing useful products.

Think about any evidence that would support this positive belief. Think about the benefits of this positive belief. Work to adapt this positive belief into your working duties

Chapter 25. Staying on course

Do not be overwhelmed

Sales can be a stressful career. There is a constant demand to meet targets. It can sometimes seem relentless. If you get several rejections one after the other it is easy to get disheartened and demoralised.

It is important not to get overwhelmed by your workload. Many activities can be delegated or rescheduled. Concentrate on the important tasks that help to keep you on target. If the workload becomes too high, enlist help or consult your boss.

Motivation and willpower

Motivation and willpower are two essential ingredients for success. Both are necessary when the going gets tough.

Remain motivated by thinking about the long-term gains from reaching your goals. Give yourself interim rewards for reaching each milestone. This will help to boost your willpower.

Set realistic targets

Set yourself realistic daily targets. Reward yourself for reaching your weekly targets.

Vary your workload

Vary your workload. This will help to keep you motivated. Break your day up into different sections. Carry out different activities in each section.

Variety helps to keep you on track and prevent burn out.

Keep a personal journal

A personal journal helps you to track your progress and learn from your experiences. Log the key events each day. Keep a note of the issues and the participants. Record your thoughts and views.

Read your personal journal or log each night. Consider:

- What went well and what could have gone better.
- Your reactions and the actions you took.
- If you should have behaved differently.
- Ways that you could have improved on your performance.
- Conflict that you could have avoided.
- If you should have taken a different approach with a customer.
- If you could have handled a prospecting telephone call better.
- How to alter your behaviour in future to get the result you want.

Review your journal each day. Regularly read old entries. Reflect on your actions. This is how you will benefit most from your experiences.

Look at the lessons that you have learned. These experiences will help you cope with unexpected situations as they arise.

Keep a log of your successes

Keep a personal log of your major successes and achievements. Refer to this log when you have experienced a setback and are beginning to doubt your abilities. This will help set things in perspective. It will give you the confidence to continue.

Do not let results control your attitude

If you keep a positive attitude you will achieve more in life. A positive attitude is the driving force behind all success.

Set your attitude at the outset. Decide that you will remain positive regardless of circumstances. Do not let results, setbacks, the mood of others or circumstances dictate your attitude. Never let unexpected results cloud your judgement.

The correct attitude will help you to maintain focus. It will enable you to persevere and hit your targets.

By being positive you will attract others to your cause. People are happy to help someone who has a positive attitude. Conversely they avoid anyone who has a negative outlook.

Recognise what you have achieved

When faced with adversity it is a good idea to pause and take stock. You may experience a run of setbacks. If this happens, just consider what you have already achieved in your career. Think about a recent sale that you closed. Remember how that made you feel. Let these recent positive feelings dispel any self-doubts that may be creeping into your mind.

Imagine what the next sale will feel like. This will give you the motivation to continue.

Imagine your regrets

Imagine your regrets if you do not meet your targets. Think about the things that you could lose out on. Think about the problems this would bring. Think about the necessary encounter with your boss.

You obviously want to avoid these eventualities, don't you? This should give you some extra motivation to continue, even when you do not feel like it.

Challenge yourself

Continually challenge yourself to do better. Look at all areas and aspects of your work.

Record what works well and what does not work. Drop anything that is not working. Repeat anything that went well. Learn from every experience. Set yourself targets for everything you do.

The comfort zone

Most people value the familiar. They stick with what they know and trust. They develop habits and routines. They mix and converse with people they know. They only feel comfortable in their own familiar environment.

These people remain in their comfort zone. They stick to the habits that they have developed. They avoid strangers and unfamiliar circumstances. They develop a fear of the unknown. They stick to a tried and trusted routine.

You must be willing to leave your comfort zone.

If you are going to succeed in sales you need to do the opposite to most people. You need to be keen to meet new people. You need to develop friendships with them and persuade them to buy your products. You need to be able to approach strangers and break the ice. You need to embrace change and variety in your working environment.

Do not avoid or delay a task because it is new and unfamiliar. Embrace new challenges. Try new methods. You need to be an instigator. Get out there and make things happen.

If you continue to use the same approach you will continue to get the same results.

The only way that you will get better results is to be willing to try something new. Never settle for the status quo. There are better methods that can be applied. You can achieve more. You just need to develop the required techniques. Keep working at it. The answers are out there.

Step outside your comfort zone

You must be willing to step outside your comfort zone in order to achieve more. Doing this helps to stretch the boundaries of your comfort zone.

Remaining within your comfort zone has the opposite effect. It causes your comfort zone to shrink in on you. People who stick to their comfort zone withdraw from more and more activities.

You will find that outside your comfort zone, all things are possible.

If you want to reach your true potential you need to step outside your comfort zone.

Self-discipline

High performers all have a high-level of self-discipline. This helps them to achieve more than everyone else.

Discipline involves making sacrifices.

Discipline involves applying more effort just when you feel like quitting. Discipline involves doing the right thing, whether you want to or not. Discipline involves doing what is required, not just what you want to do. Discipline involves the sacrifice of short-term benefits for long-term rewards.

The best way to maintain self-discipline is to set personal goals and targets. Goals promote intrinsic motivation. This motivation will help you to overcome obstacles and setbacks. It will help to boost your willpower. It will give you the strength to continue onwards when many others turn back. Winners stick to the task while others quit.

Promoting self-discipline

To help promote self-discipline:

- Plan for every event.
- Keep long-term goals in your mind.
- Develop a routine of daily targets.
- Challenge yourself in all areas.
- Set time limits on tasks.
- Stick to your schedule.
- Break larger tasks down into smaller, more manageable tasks.
- Avoid distraction and interruptions.
- Avoid negative people.
- Read self-help books.
- Become proactive rather than reactive.
- Avoid procrastination.

Discipline is all in the mind

You must appreciate that discipline is all in the mind. Discipline requires you to think in a certain manner. You can carry out certain mental exercises to improve discipline.

Visualise achieving your goals.

Visualise the benefits that will accrue. Imagine how this will feel. Focus your mind on the positive outcome. If you value the rewards over the cost then discipline will be easier to maintain.

The way to close enough sales is to get enough referrals and to find enough prospects. You must gather enough prospects and feed them into the sales funnel. You must then invest the time to establish contact, meet the prospects, find out their needs and wants, present your products and close the sale. All of this activity requires discipline and perseverance. Always keep the end goal in mind.

If you want to succeed then you must persevere when others have given up.

Selling is not a sprint activity. It is more akin to a long-distance race. In order to win the secret is not to slow down. The job is all about stamina and perseverance. The race is not won in the first ten yards. To win you need to get to the finishing line. You need to close the deal.

People do not just fail. They quit when things get tough. They throw in the towel. They lose the will to continue. You must be different. When you feel like quitting you must decide to give it one more try. You will be told 'No' many times. But if you persevere the customer might just say 'Yes' next time around.

The higher you set your targets, the bigger the rewards will be. However the obstacles will be more numerous. It will take more effort to overcome them. You will have more setbacks than the average non achiever. The difference is that you will not stop at the obstacles. You will get past them. You will achieve more than you could have thought possible.

Consistency of approach, self-discipline, patience and a positive outlook will help you achieve the success you want.

Maintain momentum

You must continue to climb up, or you will inevitably slide back. In sales you need to take action each day to move towards your goals.

Daily targets are essential. You need to maintain your momentum in the right direction. You need to reinforce the right habits.

By repeating what works each day, it becomes less daunting. Eventually it becomes second nature. You develop positive habits. Your results improve with repeated practice. You excel.

Keep to your commitments

Keeping to your commitments will help you to stay on course. If you promise to deliver by a certain date make sure that you do so. Build a reputation with your customers for delivering on time.

The more you look after your customers, the more they will look after you.

If you do not let your customers down they will return for more business.

Chapter 26. Dealing with the competition

Know your competition

Find out as much as possible about the competition. Gather the following information on all of your major competitors:

- Their products, including their features, strengths and weaknesses.
- Their market share.
- Their main customers.
- Accounts that you have taken from them.
- Accounts that they have taken from you.
- Customers who buy from both you and a competitor.
- Their sales literature, brochures, branding, advertising information and programs.
- Their core strengths and weaknesses.
- Their pricing.
- Their main selling strategy and techniques.
- Their development plans.
- The quality of their after sales service.

Your company should regularly buy the new offerings from the competition. They should then look at the new features, benefits, advertising, pricing, etc.

Position your offering

Benchmark your products against the competition. Draw up a comparison list of the features and benefits of your product versus the competition. You can use this as a sales tool in the right circumstances.

Know the strengths of your products in comparison to those of the competition. Point this out to customers.

Talking about the competition

Never criticise the competition. Just say that competition is healthy. It raises the bar for everyone. It results in better products.

Show respect for the competition, while pointing out where your product is superior. Simply differentiate your offering by concentrating on your strengths. Give testimonials of customers who switched allegiance to your company because of your superior offering.

If you criticise the competition to someone already dealing with them you are questioning their judgement. They already have an established relationship with your competitor. They will not appreciate you criticising someone whom they regard as a partner and friend.

Chapter 27. Looking after existing customers

The value of existing customers

Your customers pay the wages and the bills. Your current customers are the lifeblood of your business. Without customers there is no business.

Strive to keep existing customers. Aim to increase your business with existing customers. It is much more cost-effective to keep an existing customer than go out and find a new one. It costs six times more effort and money to get a new customer than to get a repeat order from an existing customer. Losing customers is therefore disastrous for your business.

Your customers should view you as being their first and only viable choice.

Your customer service should be so good that your customers would not even consider going anywhere else.

You have invested a great deal of time in developing trust and rapport with existing customers. Your customers have shown trust, confidence and commitment in you and your service. They have got to know, like and respect you.

Your existing customers will be much more responsive to new offerings than complete strangers would be. In addition you know the credit risk with your current customer.

Keeping existing customers should be your number one concern.

To keep your customers, keep them happy.

Both parties have made a commitment. It is up to you to keep the relationship moving forward. If you do nothing, the relationship will stagnate. You could lose the business. Keep in regular contact with your customers. Look after their concerns.

Get their CEO on board

When you open a significant new account try to get access to their CEO.

The CEO has the ultimate buying decision. Therefore they will be approached by your competitors. They will offer lower prices or introductory deals. To block these attempts you need to build rapport with the CEO.

Attend a function with your own company CEO and get him to invite the customer's CEO to come along. Make sure that you cover the benefits of your offering and the potential for developments with the customer's CEO. Get both CEO's to discuss the possibility of long term commitments and perhaps a partnership arrangement.

Build a barrier to the entry of the competition.

You must create a shield that the competition cannot penetrate. You can only do this by providing an overall service that is unrivalled.

Developing a partnership

Many large companies develop a partnership with their main or preferred suppliers. Tasks and functions are outsourced to suppliers. This can involve whole functions such as catering, security, customer service, purchasing or maintenance. With outsourcing, the supplier almost becomes part of the client's organization.

A lot of time and effort goes into setting up this relationship. However it often proves profitable for both parties. The rewards are usually a long-term relationship that is not easily decoupled. With a partnership your company is protected from the actions of your competitors. They cannot easily overcome the barrier your partnership has erected.

Your customer database

Your customer list is your most precious asset. Your customer list is your source of repeat business for existing and new products.

Gather as much personal information as possible. Record the customer's contact details and buying history. Record the buyers' likes and dislikes, their interests, their views and any other information that will help you to build rapport. Become friends with your customers if you want to secure repeat business. Keep this information up to date.

Build relationships

Have a strategy for developing your relationship with each customer. Develop a plan of action for increasing the volume of business with each customer. Set relationship targets for each customer.

Your main challenge is to keep all of your existing customers and not to lose them to the competition.

Never be complacent about your relationships with a customer.

Never make assumptions about customer loyalty. You need to be proactive. Provide a personal service that is second to none. Provide more than is expected.

Relationships must be cultivated. You must maintain regular contact with each customer. Do not simply turn up the next time you are due to take an order. A strong relationship with your existing customer erects a barrier that prevents the competition from getting the business.

Seek to broaden the relationship. Supply products to other areas of the customer's business. This will build more loyalty to your company. This makes it more difficult for the competition to get a foothold with your customer.

Your customer's needs may change with time. Keep yourself updated with your customer's needs, desires and priorities. Alter your service to meet these evolving needs.

Deliver on promises

The best way to build lasting relationships is to deliver on *all* your promises to *all* your customers *all the* time. Reputation builds relationships like nothing else. Reputation leads to referrals. Word-of-mouth is the best form of advertising. Service is everything when it comes to building goodwill.

Constantly cater to your customer's needs

Happy customers are loyal customers.

Your relationship with your customers is unique. It cannot be replicated by the competition.

Great customer care does not cost much. However, the benefits it reaps are priceless. Great customer care is not an option. It is a must.

Your customer will weigh up the verbal promises of the competition versus the experience of your service. If your service is excellent they will opt to remain with you. Actions speak louder than words.

Communicate with your customers

Communicate with your customers as often as you can. The best form of communication is face-to-face. However this method is time-consuming. Therefore you need to talk on the phone regularly. Communicating by phone is the next best method of building rapport. You should also communicate using letters, emails and personal notes.

Occasions when you can communicate

Keep in regular contact with your customers. Ring them up when they have received a large order. Ask them if there are any problems or issues.

Follow up with every customer at least once each month. Do this whether they have bought something or not. Talk to larger customers every week if not every day.

Do not abandon a customer once you have made a sale. Do not wait until it is time to get the next order before you contact them again. They will assume that you are only interested in their business and not them as a person. Take time to talk to your customers. Listen to their concerns.

Ring customers up and tell them about special offers, product updates, new products, new brochures, etc. Keep them informed about articles or other issues that might be of interest to them. Keeping in regular contact shows that you care about your customers. It shows that you appreciate their business and do not take it for granted.

Take your larger customers out to lunch or dinner when you are visiting. Send birthday and Christmas cards and a small gift. Send them tickets to a concert or event that they have expressed an interest in. Arrange to take them as your guests.

Another idea is to have a customer of the month. Arrange a special event to celebrate this.

Reasons to contact customers

Think of reasons or excuses to contact your customers. If you do not keep yourself visible the competition will try to poach your customers. Possible reasons include:

- Checking delivery of an order.
- Thanking them for an order.
- Telling them about a promotion or sale.
- Thanking them for a referral.
- Confirming attendance at a proposed meeting.
- Product updates.
- Product launches.
- New product brochures.
- Competitor information.
- A sales lead for them.
- An invite to a function.
- An invite to lunch or dinner.
- Updated prices.
- A quote.
- To issue a new contract.
- To answer a query.
- To congratulate them for some achievement.
- To remind them of a deadline.
- To show an interesting article.

Use all of these reasons and any more that you can think about to keep in regular contact with your current customers.

Communicating in writing

There will be times when you need to communicate in writing with your customers. Do this in a professional manner while keeping a personal touch.

Avoid using obvious templates and wording. Your customer does not want to receive a standard mass circulated letter from you. Take the time to handwrite your letters or notes. Your customer will appreciate the personal touch.

Keep the following guidelines in mind:

- Address your customer by his first name.
- Have a clear objective.
- Do not try to sell anything in a letter.
- Get to the point right away.
- If you need the customer to take action include this in the first two sentences.
- Use clear concise language.
- Keep the letter and the paragraphs short.
- Use bullet points to make it easy to read.
- Use a friendly tone.
- Personalise the message.
- Ask for a response if you need one.
- Double check the spelling.
- Sign off with your first name.

Establish expectations

When you secure a new customer find out their expectations early on. Understand the level and format of service the customer expects.

Interact with the customer in the manner that they prefer.

Find out the customer's preferred method of communication:

- Do they prefer to have everything in writing?
- Would they prefer that you phone them and discuss issues first?
- How often do they want you to keep in touch?

- When does late delivery become a serious problem?
- How should you deal with priority orders?
- How would they like complaints to be handled?
- Would they prefer to correct any invoicing problems directly with your accounts department?
- How much technical support would they like?
- Would they prefer to deal with routine supply issues with your customer services department?
- Would they prefer to come to you only if there is a more serious problem?

Treat all customers the same

The Pareto ratio shows that you will get 80 percent of your business from 20 percent of your customers.

You need to invest more time and effort in developing relationships with your larger customers. However you cannot ignore your smaller customers. Remember that large oaks from little acorns grow. Treat all customers the same, regardless of how much they spend. The small spender today could become the big spender tomorrow.

You would be surprised how quickly things can change. Businesses do not need to grow organically. Mergers and acquisitions can mean that buying habits alter radically almost overnight.

All customers are entitled to the same excellent level of service. This holds, regardless of their size or budget. Take time to find out how all of your customers prefer to do business. Tailor your service to their needs.

Friendly personal service and attention to detail is what keeps customers coming back for more.

Have multiple contacts

Make sure that you have more than one contact with your customers. You do not want to lose your business because a regular buyer leaves the company. Have multiple contacts with your bigger customers. Take the time to build rapport and get to know each of these contacts.

Always get to know the more junior people supporting the buyer. It is more than likely that his replacement will come from this source. You can do this when visiting larger customers. Invite them out for lunch with the buyer. Make notes later of the personal interests and goals of these people. Drop this information into later conversations.

Understand your customer's organization

Get to know your customer's organization. You may find opportunities in other departments and branches. Get to know who has the decision making authority. Whose opinion do manager's trust? Who has the ability to influence others? Which contacts should you nurture?

Talk to the users

Talk to the end users of your products. Get feedback on how the products perform. Get their suggestions for improvements.

Find out if any other products from your range would be of benefit. Make sure that you build rapport with the end users. The buyer will often ask their opinion before contacting suppliers.

Learn something new

Learn something new about existing customers every time that you visit them. The more you learn about your customer's concerns, interests and requirements the better. Keep on the lookout for new opportunities with existing customers.

Use quiet periods

Use quieter periods such as holidays to send updated information to customers.

Chapter 28. Customer service

Provide great service

Great service is what brings customers back time and again. If you can provide great service you will set yourself and your company apart from the competition.

Why not provide something extra or unexpected for the customer. The holiday firm that provides a champagne reception for guests booking into their hotel does just that. People talk about this unexpected treat to their friends. It generates repeat business from the customer and extra business from their friends and family.

Golden rules for customer service

Providing excellent customer service will pay huge dividends to any business. Word of mouth promotion is much more successful than any other form of advertising.

- Treat every customer as you would like to be treated yourself.
- Be reliable, honest and trustworthy in all of your customer dealings.
- Make sure that the first impression you give is a good one.
- Smile and remain positive and enthusiastic when dealing with customers.
- Anticipate your customer's needs.
- Take time to get to know your customers.
- Find out your customer's needs and wants.
- Keep a record of all of your customer's wants, needs and interests.
- Thank your customers for giving you their business.
- Follow up with your customers after every sale and delivery.
- Ask your customers how you could improve your service.

- Use suggestion cards for feedback.
- Acknowledge all feedback from customers.
- Keep in regular contact with your customers.
- Remember that you are selling yourself as well as your products.
- Let your customers know about new products, sales, promotions or deals.
- Make it easy for your customers to say yes.
- Under promise and over deliver.
- Exceed your customer's expectations.
- Build a reputation for excellent service.
- Make reliability your watchword.
- Provide value for money.
- Tailor your service to each customer's specific needs.
- Make it easy for customers to contact you.
- Do not make your customers deal with an answer service.
- Answer the phone promptly and give the customer your undivided attention.
- Smile when you answer the phone.
- Deal with all queries at once.
- Deal with all problems promptly and to the customer's satisfaction.
- If problems arise, let the customer know right away and agree a course of action.
- Keep your customer informed of progress when dealing with problems.
- Continually look at ways of improving your service.
- Shorten your delivery times.
- Send birthday cards and Christmas cards to your customers.
- Never become complacent.
- Never take custom for granted.
- Acknowledge and reward customer loyalty.
- Always be punctual for meetings with customers.

How your company can facilitate customer service

- Set standards for customer care.
- Include your customer service number on your invoices.
- Include your customer service contact details on the company web site.
- Have real people answer the phones.
- Become a member of a recognised trade or professional association.
- Have a user-friendly web site.
- Use high quality sales brochures and supporting literature.
- Have flexible opening hours that suit your customer's needs.
- Regularly develop new products.
- Have seasonal offerings.
- Have a strict ethical code in all customer dealings.
- Develop partnerships with suppliers and customers.
- Manage the availability of your product lines.
- Ensure that product quality is to specification.
- Develop a reputation for excellent customer service.
- Work to best environmental standards.
- Exceed your customer's expectations.
- Carry out thorough market research to identify changing customer needs.
- Provide excellent facilities for customers who visit your site.
- Instruct every employee on the importance of customer service.
- Train all staff dealing with customers to the highest standards.
- Have excellent buildings and facilities if operating in a retail environment
- Provide for customers who have special needs.
- Benchmark company performance against competitors.

Customer care standards

Your company should set standards for customer care and service. Anyone dealing directly with customers should be trained to meet these standards.

Set standards for:

- Answering and dealing with customer phone calls.
- Dealing with email requests from customers.
- Meeting with customers.
- Dealing with customer complaints.
- Delivery of product.

Set standards for how promptly employees answer queries. If a customer has more than one query then address all of their concerns in your initial answer.

Set standards on how to forward complaints to the relevant people. There should be standards for communicating with customers. Set maximum time limits before appropriate action is taken.

Your standards should be specific and measurable. Record actual performance against the standards. For example your delivery standard could be that you guarantee next working day delivery within the UK mainland. Take corrective action if you fail to meet your standards. This may be in the form of additional training, improved facilities or new procedures.

The importance of accuracy

Make sure that you collect accurate customer information. This will avoid problems when dealing with orders. Always double check spelling of names and addresses.

After meeting with a customer send an email confirming the agreed course of action. Include the order details, amount charged and expected delivery dates. When you take an order leave a copy of the order and delivery details with the customer. This way there should be no misunderstandings.

Researching customer needs and perceptions

Your company should regularly review customer needs and perceptions. This will provide the feedback you need to improve service levels.

The customer's perceptions are reality for them.

Your customer's perception may not be what you want it to be. If this is the case you need to improve your service levels. Words alone will not change your customer's perceptions. It will require action on your part. You will need to correct the problem and remove the causes. This is the only way to change perceptions.

The common methods of gathering customer information include:

- Customer comment cards.
- Customer focus groups.
- Mystery shoppers.
- Market research.
- Opinion surveys.
- Customer panels.
- Product user groups.

Questions you should ask include:

- How did you found out about our products or service?
- Which products do you currently buy from us?
- How often do you buy from us?
- How often do you buy from competitors?
- What is the most important thing for you when dealing with our company?
- What do you expect from our company?

- How well do our products and service meet your expectations?
- Have you experienced any problems with our products or service?
- Do you have any suggestions to improve our service?
- How will your needs change in the future?

For each question you ask, give the customer space to write out their answer and any comments. Also give them the chance of rating your service from poor through to excellent.

Questionnaires should only take a few minutes at most to complete. They should not be longer than a single page. They should be limited to 8 or 9 questions.

If some cases, surveys need to be longer and more detailed. Offer an incentive if you want people to take the time to complete them. This incentive may be a discount voucher or a free entry into a prize draw.

Customer surveys are of no use unless you act on them.

It is pointless carrying out customer surveys if you fail to act on them. In fact it can be counter productive. If you ask the customer how you can improve your service and then ignore their answer you will send the wrong signal.

Do not stop at gathering customer information. Analyse it and act on it. Use the information to improve your procedures.

Publish the results of any surveys and send a copy to anyone who took part

Provide feedback to everyone who has completed the survey. Tell them how you have altered and improved your service based on their suggestions.

What do you get from giving this feedback? The chances are you will have secured a customer for life and referrals to their friends and family.

The importance of the mystery shopper

All staff dealing with customers must always behave in a professional, attentive, polite and helpful manner.

Imagine if just one member of staff is having a bad day. Their negative demeanour and behaviour will send out the wrong impression of the complete company.

If a customer has a bad experience with one member of staff he will assume that your company does not care about customer service. The customer will take his business elsewhere. Worse still he will tell all his friends, family, work colleagues and acquaintances about the experience.

No matter how well you train and supervise staff, you cannot stand over them 100 percent of the time. However you need to ensure that they behave in the proper manner when you are not around. One way of doing this is to employ the service of a mystery shopper.

A mystery shopper is someone you know or employ who goes undercover and adapts the role of a customer. They then provide you with feedback on their experiences.

The mystery shopper can give feedback on:

- How long they waited before being acknowledged and greeted.
- The length of any queues.
- The friendliness and attentiveness of staff.
- How well the staff performed in taking care of their needs.
- The accuracy of the information they received.
- The speed of the service.

- The help they received with any problems.
- The appearance and attitude of staff.
- The general cleanness of the surroundings.

If your employees know that you employ mystery shoppers then there is a greater chance that they will behave appropriately in all of their customer dealings.

Also employ positive methods of rewarding your employees for providing excellent customer service. Have an employee of the month award based on customer feedback.

Chapter 29. Dealing with customer complaints

Welcome customer complaints

Welcome customer complaints and deal with them at once. Do everything you can to resolve the complaint to the customer's satisfaction as quickly as possible. Investigate and get back to the customer. Discuss the options and agree what needs to be done.

Make sure the customer knows that you are giving their complaint top priority. Then rectify the problem.

When a customer complains you have the opportunity of putting things right and satisfying the customer's needs. You will then be able to retain the customer.

Disgruntled customers

It is a much more serious problem when the customer does not complain. Many people do not want to complain directly to the person providing the service.

Most people wish to avoid confrontation.

Many people will leave a restaurant if the meal was poor without complaining. They do not want to confront the staff involved. However dissatisfied customers will readily talk to others about the poor service levels. Dissatisfied customers tell about twenty times as many people as happy customers do.

Bad news spreads much faster than good news.

Disgruntled customers complain to friends, family and other potential customers. This harms your reputation and your business. Dissatisfied customer will go elsewhere in the future. Often you are unaware of this. You certainly will not know the reason. You are not given the chance to fix the problem.

Make sure that your staff ask every customer about their experiences before they leave your premises. If they are not happy then apologise and try to rectify the situation.

Respond immediately

Respond immediately to all complaints. Complaint handling should be the number one priority of everyone in your business.

Everything else can wait.

Retaining customers should be top priority in every company. All complaints should be dealt with as quickly and as efficiently as possible. They should be dealt with to the customer's satisfaction. Even if you lose money dealing with the complaint it is much more important to keep the customer.

A satisfied customer is a repeat customer.

Give employees authority to act

Cut out the red tape when dealing with complaints. Give individual employees the authority to make instant decisions. Let them and use their discretion within recognised guidelines. This speeds up the response time in dealing with customer complaints.

Calming customers down

Sometimes you need to calm customers down before you can help deal with their problem.

You may feel that a customer is overreacting to what is a minor problem. However you do not know the history. This may not be the first time the customer has experienced a problem. They may not be happy with the way their previous problems were dealt with.

The way to calm a customer down is to lead and control their body language. An angry customer will raise their voice. They will speak faster than normal. Their breathing rate will have increased.

Express indignation that they have had such a problem. Then say that it is not typical of your company's service. Do this with a slightly raised voice and talk slightly faster than normal. Mirroring their body language leads the customer to believe that you appreciate the seriousness of the situation for them. You are displaying empathy. You are on their side.

Next slow down the rate of your speech, slow your breathing and gradually drop the volume. Do all this while explaining that you will look into this immediately. You will personally deal with the problem. You just need to first jot down all the details. Promise that you will not rest until the problem has been resolved to their satisfaction. You then smile and ask them to explain exactly what has occurred.

This technique leads the customer away from an emotional state where confrontation is likely. It takes them towards a more rational state of mind. This way you can deal with the problem to their satisfaction. The result is that you keep a valued customer.

Give something back

If a customer makes a genuine complaint and has been inconvenienced, then offer something back.

Obviously you will have to replace faulty or damaged equipment. Go beyond your commitments. Give something extra to show that you care. You could offer an extended warranty on the replacement. You could offer a discount on the next purchase. You could give the customer some free vouchers.

Follow up

Follow up a few days later. Make sure the customer is satisfied with how you have dealt with the complaint. If not, do what you can to fix the problem.

Complaint handling guidelines

Use the following guidelines in dealing with customer complaints:

- Your number one aim is to retain the customer.
- It does not matter if the customer is right or wrong. It is the customer's perception that matters.
- Take personal ownership of the problem and deal with it for the customer.
- Do not pass the customer from pillar to post.
- Immediately acknowledge the problem.
- Empathise with the customer.
- Listen carefully to the full complaint.
- Do not interrupt or make assumptions.
- Agree where you can.
- Do not argue or take an opposing stance.
- Take notes. Echo back what the customer has said.
- Get the customer to confirm your understanding of the problem.
- Assure the customer that you will personally deal with their complaint.
- Apologise and take responsibility for rectifying the situation.
- Agree on a resolution that will satisfy the customer. Give alternative choices if possible.
- Resolve the problem immediately if possible.
- If the problem cannot be resolved immediately, then agree a time frame and stick to it.
- Give something back, above and beyond what was agreed.

- Contact the customer and check the problem has been resolved to their satisfaction.
- Review the complaint and how it was handled.
- Initiate procedures to prevent the problem happening again.

Review complaint handling procedures

Every time a customer complains find out what went wrong. First check that the complaint was handled correctly. If not look at what needs to happen in future.

Look for permanent solutions to the problem.

Always seek to introduce procedures to avoid the situation recurring. This is how you make permanent improvements to your service.

Log customer complaints and keep a record of them. Over time you will build up a history. This data will point to areas where your company must improve facilities, procedures or equipment. Act on this information. Aim to be the best. Discerning customers choose the best every time.

Chapter 30. Key account management

You need to employ a logical and detailed method of managing key accounts.

Personal information to gather on customers

Gather certain personal information on all of your customers, including:

- Their birthday.
- Their home town.
- Where they live.
- Their hobbies.
- Their interests.
- Their favourite restaurant.
- Their college or university.
- Their children's names.
- The make of their car.
- Their favourite sports team.
- Where they last went on holidays.
- The last place they worked.
- Their favourite film or book.

This personal information will enable you to build rapport and improve relationships with your customers. Always relate to your customers on their level. Talk about what concerns and interests them.

Information to gather on you customer's business

- Location of their headquarters, branches, factories, warehouses, etc.
- Details of any subsidiaries or partners.
- Their main organization chart.

- Annual accounts information such as sales turnover and profits.
- Their market share.
- Your share of the customer's purchasing budget.
- The customer's share of your total sales.
- Planned investments and expansion plans.
- Personal information on all the key decision makers.
- Their buying approval policy.
- Their pricing and discount policy.
- Their visitor policy.
- Their entertainment and gift receipt policy.
- Their return on capital employed.
- Their return on sales.
- Their profit by product category and market category.

This information will enable you to appreciate the relative importance of each account. It will also indicate how important your business is to the customer. It will help ensure that you interact with the customer in a manner that complies with their established procedures.

Chapter 31. Sales tools and documentation

Use the following documentation and tools to help sell your products or service. Every tool or aid that you use should be high quality, new and in pristine condition.

Samples

You need mock-ups and working samples of your products for demonstrations. You may also need diagrams and schematics to help explain how the product works.

Endorsements

You will need typed endorsements from satisfied customers. The more prestigious the company or the individual involved the better.

Independent product reviews

Independent product reviews are a great help in building confidence in your products and your company.

Marketing material

Your marketing department will produce annual or seasonal brochures. They will also run advertising campaigns. They may have product or advertising DVDs. They could have results from customer satisfaction surveys. All of this and other statistics and material they produce can be of use in securing the sale.

Referrals

Referrals are a great door opener. Referrals help to buy you the few minutes you need on that cold call to make your pitch.

Freebies

Leave freebies with your company name and an advertising logo. This keeps your company name to the fore front of the buyers mind.

Tickets

Tickets to events such as concerts or the theatre are a great way of building rapport with customers. It is better to go with the customer when they attend the event.

Suggest that your company buys corporate season tickets to a sports stadium such as a local football team. Your sales team could take different clients to home games throughout the season.

Factory tours

Invite potential customers to come and see your facilities. What better way of building confidence in your products and your company?

Product comparison charts

Have comparison charts drawn up for all of your products. Benchmark them against the equivalent competitor products in each case.

Use comparison charts as an aid to selling the product. Use them to prevent customers from shopping around. There will be no point in them wasting time and effort looking elsewhere if they can immediately see that your product offers the best value for money.

Wine and dine

Meet customers for breakfast, lunch or dinner. It enables you to leave the distractions of the office behind and build rapport. It allows you to find out more about the person and any common interests. If you want to sell more to someone then you need to become their friend. You need to be seen to be just like them.

Networking

Networking at industry events, road shows, professional dinners and charity events are all great ways of building rapport and gathering new leads.

Chapter 32. Leading a sales team

Definition of leadership

Your role as a leader is to lead others in the spirit of your vision. Have a vision for your department and communicate this to your team.

Develop a positive energy. Display enthusiasm for everything that you do. This will help to inspire and motivate others. You must have a winning attitude and seek positive outcomes.

Your role is to be forward thinking. You need to plan for future events. Your role is to set the direction that your team will take. Set the tempo for change.

Aim to get your team to work harder. Under your supervision they should achieve more than they would have done if left to their own devices. To do this, create an environment where people can flourish.

> *As a leader your job is to produce results through the efforts of others.*

Build respect and trust. This enables others to perform to the best of their ability. Inspire every member of your team to follow you.

The role of the leader

Your role in leading a successful sales team is to:

- Provide common objectives and goals for your team.
- Keep the team working together as a cohesive group.
- Support each team member in order to gain optimum team performance.

Provide direction

Provide the vision for the future. Set the long-term goals for your team. Define their overall tasks. Set short-term objectives. These should contribute towards achieving longer term goals.

Initiate change

Your job is to facilitate and implement change. You must be an instigator and a champion of causes. You must be proactive.

Results oriented

You will be judged on your results. Focus on results. Teach your sales team to think likewise. Activity does not guarantee achievement. There is a difference between being busy and being productive.

Always keep the end result in mind in all of your dealings. Results, not effort alone, bring success. Set rewards based on achieving results.

Make a positive difference

Make a positive difference to those around you. Influence how people feel about their work.

Aim to create an environment of trust, camaraderie and understanding. Help people to enjoy their work.

Communication

Communication, especially the ability to listen is a must in sales management. Good communication builds relationships. Good relationships lead to success. Build trust through constructive working relationships. Aim to help, influence and engage others.

Talk to your customers regularly. Find out if they are satisfied with the service provided by your sales team. The feedback will let you know how your team is performing.

Get to know the individual needs of each member of your sales team. Answer their queries. Explain their role in contributing towards the overall company objectives.

Provide your team with regular updates. Explain how they are contributing to the overall success of the company.

Intrinsic leadership qualities

Leading a team takes time. It involves acquiring certain skills and experience.

If you want to lead others you must regularly analyse your personal behaviour. Continually strive to alter it for the better.

Aim to improve your interpersonal skills. This will help to get the optimum performance from each member of your sales team.

Vision

As a sales leader you need vision and foresight. You need to plan ahead. You must charter the way for others. You must give your sales team a sense of direction, meaning and purpose. Your team should know where they currently are, where they are going and how they will get there. They must understand their own individual roles and how they can contribute to overall team success.

Values

You need to develop a set of values. These values will be your moral compass. They will guide you to your ultimate destiny. Consider those issues that are important to you. There are certain principles that you should not compromise on.

You should recognise and clarify your values. Embed these values into your behaviour. The choices you make in life will be influenced by your core values and beliefs. Remain true to yourself.

All too often it is tempting to go for that easy close. Do not do this if what you are selling is not what the customer needs. Take the time and provide them with what they want.

Think about what is important to you. Then write down your top ten most important values. Typical values might be:

- I will always be honest with myself and others.
- I will encourage and respect the views and contributions of others.
- I will treat everyone equally and fairly.
- I will recognise my own limitations.
- I will deliver on all of my promises.
- I will recognise and accept diversity in others.
- I will not tolerate prejudice in myself or others.
- I will continually aim to learn something new.
- I will always look for the good in others.
- I will always listen carefully to others and show empathy.
- I will develop my team to the best of my ability.
- I will maintain a positive attitude.

Think about your behaviour. Think about how you treat others. Convey your values to each member of your sales team. They must understand your principles. They must know where you will not compromise.

Your values are more important than your possessions.

Losing sight of your values will cost much more than losing your possessions. You can replace lost possessions easily. However if you lose your integrity or reputation it can be a daunting task to rebuild it.

Courage

Have the courage to deal with conflict and other difficult situations. Stand up for your values and beliefs. Take the right course of action. Always do what you feel is right. Maintain your core values in all circumstances.

Do not let your own wants and needs override the needs of others.

You must do what is right for the customer first and foremost.

Clearly understand what is ethically and morally right and what is wrong.

Self-confidence

Self-confidence is an essential leadership attribute. Have confidence in your abilities. You should possess emotional stability and self-assurance.

People respond to what they see and experience. Appear and act in a self-confident manner. This will build trust and belief in your capacity as a leader. It will help you to gain the commitment of each member of your team.

Enthusiasm

You need to be passionate, enthusiastic and energetic in your role.

Enthusiasm is infectious. It helps to motivate others. Your sales team will always pick up on your mood as their leader.

Self-discipline

It takes an abundance of self-discipline to lead a sales team. You will need self-discipline to overcome setbacks and persevere when things are not going as expected. You will have your own problems and those of each member of your team to resolve and overcome.

Make a difference in everything you do and to everyone you meet.

As a leader you need to develop a strong work ethic. You must go beyond what is expected and what is required. You must set yourself apart. Lead by example. Others will follow.

Accountability

As a sales leader you will be held accountable for the results and behaviour of yourself and your team. You must accept responsibility and accountability for the performance of your team.

You are responsible for any failures.

Commitment is a two-way street. You cannot shift the blame onto your team when things go wrong. By accepting personal accountability for all failings you will build trust and respect with your sales team.

Give your team the credit when things go well and take the blame when they don't.

Catch your employees doing something right and praise them in the presence of others.

Awareness

You need to develop your self-awareness. Know your strengths and weaknesses. Also know the strengths and weaknesses of each member of your sales team.

Be aware of what motivates others. Understand what each situation demands.

Take time to observe how successful salespeople get results by interacting with others. Also notice how others fail to get the results they wanted. Note what was different in their approach. Look at which techniques worked and which failed. Learn from your observations.

Pass this experience onto your team.

Integrity

Leadership demands character.

You need integrity in order to build trust with your sales team. You must be authentic and genuine. Be open and honest with others. Do as you promise. Keep your word. Practise what you preach.

Reliability is crucial when dealing with customers. You cannot promise one thing and deliver another. Do as you say and say as you do. Do not pay lip service to your ideals. Honour all of your commitments.

Always check available resources before making a commitment. Be certain that you can deliver when promised. Do not offer excuses for unreliability.

Treat people with respect. Make yourself available to your team. Be consistent in your demands. Communicate clearly with others. Do not get involved with gossip, office politics and complaining about others.

Treat every member of your team in the same manner, regardless of their rank. Show dignity and respect for others. Be patient with your team. Recognise their limits and seek to develop their potential. Be loyal to your team. Never divulge information that you have received in confidence.

Support your team with their concerns. Represent their interests to senior management. These are the actions that will help build trust with your sales team.

Respect the feelings and opinions of your team. Be open to opposing viewpoints.

Decisiveness

Make prompt decisions once you have gathered the right information and consulted with interested parties. If you cannot do this you will hamper the effectiveness of your team.

Sign off on proposed action promptly. Give ready access to yourself. Do not delay your team when decisions need to be made.

Delegate responsibility where you can. Let your team members make their own decisions within certain guidelines.

Open-minded approach

Leadership is not a dominion over others. Do not be an autocrat.

> ***You must be as open to bad news as you are to good news.***

Do not surround yourself with yes-men. Remain open-minded. Listen to advice, feedback and suggestions. However it is your responsibility to make the final decision based on the available facts.

You do not know it all. Recognise your current level of knowledge. Strive to learn more about your organization, your team, your products, your role and most of all your customers.

Humility

You need to have a degree of humility. Be aware of your own limitations. Be prepared to learn from others. If you win in a particular situation, make sure that you win with grace.

Acknowledge the contribution of your team. Never indulge in bragging. Nothing turns people off quicker.

If you do not listen to others you will learn little of value.

Never act in a superior manner with your team or your customers. Listen if others are advising that you are taking the wrong path. Your team will be closer to their individual customers. They often know the right course of action in any given circumstance.

Encourage participation

Ask for ideas and suggestions from your team. Make sure that everyone has an input at sales meetings.

Focus on collaboration rather than confrontation or competition.

Common solutions will help others to buy into your proposals.

Building relationships

Build and nurture relationships if you want to succeed. Trust is the cornerstone on which all relationships are built. Build this trust with each member of your team, with co-workers and with your customers.

Delegating

Concentrate on the important tasks. Delegate as much administrative work as possible. Delegate as much responsibility to your team members as possible.

Define the acceptable standards of work. Ensure the tasks are clearly understood. Develop the skills and confidence of each team member. Then let them get on with things.

Delegate progressively more challenging tasks to each team member. This will enable them to gain experience and confidence.

Organizing

Organise individuals and resources to achieve each objective.

Success in sales requires excellent time management and organizing skills. You must make every hour and every day count.

Controlling

Control the output of your sales team. Keep everyone on track. Set the tempo.

Define the acceptable standards of behaviour and performance. Measure the performance of each team member. Provide feedback and let them know if they are hitting their targets.

Prod and encourage others as needed to help achieve the team goals. At times you will have to let individuals know that they need to improve their performance.

Training

Provide the best training you can get. Have your sales team attend seminars and workshops. Put trainees working alongside experienced colleagues. They can learn skills such as building rapport or closing sales.

Coaching

Coach your team if you want to improve their performance. To lead a team you must adapt a different role from the team players. Your function is to guide, motivate, support and encourage your team to achieve common goals and objectives.

Support each team member by instilling trust, listening to concerns and providing feedback, advice and guidance. Give feedback on performance and advice on how to improve it.

Help your team members to do things for themselves. Look to continually gain small improvements in individual performance. This will collectively add up to big improvements in team performance. It is the little things that make the difference in the long run.

Motivating

A key role in sales leadership is motivation. You need to motivate each individual team member. This enables the team as a whole to achieve its targets.

You need to manage the emotions of others to get the best performance from them. If people feel good about themselves then they will improve their decision making, energy levels, behaviour and performance.

Representing

Represent the interests of your sales team to senior management. Defend the group against attack from other departments if necessary.

You must also represent the interests of the organization to your team. Champion initiatives aimed at improvements. Support any new company policy as if it where your own.

The leader as role model

As a leader you must act as a role model for your sales team. Others will observe how you behave. They will model their behaviour on yours. They will mirror your actions. If you want them to be positive, enthusiastic and motivated, then you need to lead by setting this example.

Removing barriers

A core part of your responsibilities will be to recognise and remove barriers to progress.

Do not constrain your team with procedures, paperwork and red tape. Team members should not need your approval for every little decision that must be taken.

Deal promptly with any problems or concerns that hamper progress. Deal immediately with any disagreements or conflict.

Set consistent goals

Be consistent in your goal setting. Be consistent in how you communicate instructions.

Avoid competing priorities. They will lead to confusion on which tasks to complete first.

Avoid shifting priorities where you give one instruction one day and issue the opposite instruction the next day.

Set achievable targets

Set achievable targets for your sales team. Agree individual targets with each employee in advance.

Targets should match the competence of the individual concerned. Include a degree of stretch to challenge the individual. Provide assistance where needed.

Allocate sufficient time and resources to your team members. This will allow them to hit their targets.

Specify standards

Specify the standards required from your team. You can keep written specifications or simply communicate the standards required when you delegate work.

You need standards to ensure that results are of the required quality.

Measure performance

Devise a means of measuring performance to ensure that targets are met. Check the performance of each salesperson on an individual customer basis.

Review performance

Review performance every week. Give praise openly where it is merited. Give private constructive feedback to individuals on how to improve performance next time.

Review conversion ratios for each member of your team. If anyone scores low in a particular area consider putting them alongside someone who scores highly in this area.

Give effective feedback

Give regular effective feedback to each team member. When they have completed an assignment for you, take time to review it with them. Ask them for their views on the work. Find out if there were any areas where they experienced difficulty. Offer advice where you can. Praise any aspects of the work that were carried out well.

Be professional in your dealings with your team. Remain calm and objective. Encourage your team to perform to their potential. This approach helps to build trust and support.

Frank debate

Hold weekly sales meetings with your team. Encourage each team member to give their honest opinion on anything that they disagree with. Ask for suggestions on anything that they think could be done better.

Look at ways of transferring success in one area or region to all other areas. Make sure that lessons learnt in one area are learned across the board.

The aim is to improve the overall effectiveness of the team. Any team activity should be open for debate. Invite everyone to give their input. By getting issues out in the open you can deal with them to the satisfaction of the team.

Create a shared vision

A shared vision provides team members with a clear sense of direction. Give individuals some scope and freedom on how to go about the tasks. People often find their own ways of getting somewhere once they know the destination.

Clarify roles

Let people know exactly what their role is. Let them know what you expect from them. They should know what to do when things are going well and what to do in adverse conditions.

Get commitment

Get commitment from each team member. Everyone must buy into each decision, regardless of whether they proposed it or not. Every member of your crew must row in the same direction.

Make targets progressively more challenging

Set progressively more challenging targets. Initial targets should be easy to achieve. By reaching these targets they will gain confidence. They will be motivated to continue.

Provide the best resources

Provide the best resources you can get for your team. Provide the best office facilities and computer equipment you can afford. Any tools or equipment should be the best that you can afford. Training should be ongoing, targeted and effective.

If you want to get the best results then make sure that resources are not an issue.

Trust your team

Trust your team to reach their targets. After you have delegated work, allow them to get on with it. Do not micromanage people.

Be open and honest with your team. Encourage them to come forward with any issues that they have. Give them the responsibility to make their own decisions.

Work to the strengths of your team

Different team members have different strengths and skills. Recognise that there are horses for courses when assigning tasks.

Get people to specialise in what they do best. This is the best way to get the optimum overall performance from your team.

Involve everyone

Involve all team members in what you are trying to achieve. Do not leave anyone out, regardless of their ability or level of enthusiasm.

Make everyone feel that they have a valid input to make. Recognise and accept their views.

Step back

Learn to step back so that others can step forward. Do not dominate discussions and meetings. Maintain control but let others give their input.

www.ingramcontent.com/pod-product-compliance
Lightning Source LLC
Chambersburg PA
CBHW051636170526
45167CB00001B/216